Contents

A world of possibilities

Inexpensive and strong, concrete holds up houses, paves driveways, and keeps fence posts from tipping over. But beyond these utilitarian roles, it also excels as a decorative material. Adding color, using special sand or gravel, and varying the surface finish change its look in nearly limitless ways. You can pour concrete into forms, sculpt it almost as if it were clay, and carve it after it is set but not yet very hard. No wonder decorative concrete is showing up in more and more houses in everything from countertops and fireplace surrounds to tabletops and garden art. Whether you tackle a project on your own or hire someone to do it, this chapter gives you the background you need to wind up with a great result.

Exploring concrete

INDOORS OR OUT, decorative concrete can play a role in your home. Looking for something different in a tub or sink? Want a striking table or bench for your patio? Concrete may give you the design options you are seeking in these situations and many more.

One of the greatest things about concrete is that it can be molded into virtually any shape and produced in virtually limitless colors or patterns. So as you peruse this book, remember that you aren't locked into the specific combinations of features that you see. Feel free to mix and match ideas as you plan decorative concrete features for your own home.

ABOVE: *Thin concrete overlays can form floors like this. Spread over plain concrete or sometimes even wooden subfloors topped with cement board, these toppings can be adorned with pigments, stains, stencils, or decorative cuts. Several techniques can be combined in a single floor.*

BELOW, LEFT: *Perhaps the ultimate soaking tub, this concrete extravagance has plenty of room for two. Some manufacturers cast tubing for radiant heat into concrete tubs, ensuring that the water stays comfortable for long periods. The tub then doubles as the heat source for the room.*

BELOW, RIGHT: *Decorative concrete techniques can turn plain paving into textured expanses that look like stone or brick.*

ABOVE: *This fireplace surround was cast with fragments of yellow glass salvaged from old traffic signals. Grinding and then polishing wore away the surface skin of cement and fine sand, revealing the sparkle of the glass. A steel I-beam serves as a mantel.*

Concrete countertops aren't cheap, but they often incorporate elements that would be far more expensive if executed with other materials. This curved countertop features a drain ramp that's perfectly sized to fit the perforated pan, which also slides over the sinks along a molded-in lip. Countertops can also accommodate cutting boards that slide in the same way.

OUTFITTING A KITCHEN

When decorative concrete began to appear indoors, it showed up first in kitchen countertops. Then came concrete sinks, floors, and tables. The first time people hear about countertops made from concrete, they tend to raise an eyebrow in skepticism. But seeing some of the possibilities turns them into believers and banishes the notion that concrete always looks as it does on a garage floor.

Concrete countertops range from about $1\frac{1}{2}$ inches thick—the standard for most countertops in the United States—to 6 inches or more. Some are simple rectangles. Others incorporate complex geometric shapes and may have special features such as molded-in drain boards. Sinks range from basic boxes to elaborate creations with curves or complex angles. With concrete, almost anything is possible.

ABOVE: *This simple blue countertop owes much to its sinuous curve. Besides adding beauty, the edge creates enough space for multiple stools in this breakfast area. The curve also cuts down on the size of the countertop, keeping it from blocking access between the family room and the kitchen.*

ABOVE, LEFT: *A concrete countertop and a matching farmhouse sink create a soothing, unified look in this kitchen. The metal insert cast into the sink helps keep the surface from chipping.*

ABOVE, RIGHT: *Kitchen counters are often long and wide, but diminutive ones have a place too. A small version is just right for a pass-through between a kitchen and a dining room.*

RIGHT: *A greenish concrete island and gray concrete floors coexist nicely with mottled yellow walls, natural-wood cabinets, and stainless steel in this kitchen. The warm feeling of the room results from more than the visual contrast, though. A radiant-heat system embedded in the floor also keeps the temperature cozy.*

OPPOSITE: *Concrete countertops often include built-in drain boards. This one has a series of grooves molded into a sloping section next to the sink. It also has a built-in trivet for hot pots. Grooves for the trivet fit metal rods that project higher than the countertop. The rods can be set in epoxy or left loose, which makes them easy to remove for cleaning.*

DESIGNING A BATHROOM

Some bathrooms are so tiny that it's difficult to fit in all the essential components. Others are so spacious that the challenge becomes finding pieces with enough heft to look like they belong. Whatever your situation, a concrete countertop, sink, or tub may solve design issues.

In powder rooms or other bathrooms with stylish flair, you can indulge in sinks with unusual forms. Where space is tight, you can design a countertop that uses every inch of available space or install a tub where a standard manufactured model won't fit. In a large bathroom, you can order a concrete tub that's as big as you want.

Be wary of opting for a tub that's too big, though. Besides requiring enormous amounts of hot water, oversize tubs weigh so much that you may need to add supports to the floor. Remember that it's not just the weight of the tub that matters. You also need to factor in the water, which weighs 8.3 pounds per gallon.

ABOVE: *Although some concrete tubs are cast in one piece, it's also possible to build them in parts that can be assembled in place—an advantage in remodeling situations and in upstairs bathrooms. This tub started as three pieces, which were then mechanically fastened and glued together for a watertight seal.*

LEFT: *Concrete tiles, marbled with white, establish a sleek, modern look in this bathroom.*

OPPOSITE, BOTTOM LEFT: *A trough sink works equally well for washing hands or lingerie.*

OPPOSITE, BOTTOM RIGHT: *Concrete allows you to have integral sinks in unique shapes and sizes.*

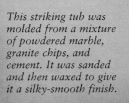

This striking tub was molded from a mixture of powdered marble, granite chips, and cement. It was sanded and then waxed to give it a silky-smooth finish.

CONCRETE FLOORS AND WALLS

Decorative concrete has worked its way into starring roles throughout the house. In floors and walls, it often serves as a structural material, though it can also be a decorative finish applied as a thin topping over wood or drywall. However it's formed, the concrete creates a beautiful surface that's easy to keep clean. Thick concrete walls and floors also tend to moderate temperatures in a house because concrete absorbs heat from sunlight that streams in through windows during the day and then radiates that heat back into the air at night.

ABOVE: *Where more texture is desired, installers often cut shallow grooves in the concrete. Depending on how the lines are laid out, this can produce the look of tile or simply result in an interesting pattern, as shown in this floor. The color comes from dyes in a range of colors.*

RIGHT: *Concrete overlay materials can also create swirling, free-form designs.*

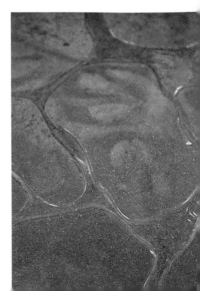

ABOVE, LEFT: *Concrete walls can be poured in place, or a thin layer can be troweled over drywall, much like venetian plaster is.*

ABOVE, RIGHT: *Pressing textured mats or rollers into concrete or concrete overlays while the material is still soft results in a slightly uneven surface that mimics natural stone. This technique also creates indented grout lines, adding to the realistic look.*

RIGHT: *There are several ways to give a concrete floor the look of tile. One way is to outline individual "tiles" with tape or another dye-resistant material and then apply stain or dye between them. This results in a smooth surface without the unevenness of actual grout lines.*

OUTFITTING LIVING ROOMS AND OTHER SPACES

In living rooms, dens, home offices, and other spaces, concrete can form stunningly beautiful fireplaces, furniture, and other details.

For fireplaces, the options include mantels, hearths, and full surrounds. Some resemble pieces that were traditionally made of stone, while others are cast into fresh shapes that look unabashedly like concrete. Thin fireplace surrounds can be installed over cement board and attached with mastic, just as tile would be. Mantels or other pieces that project from the wall must be bolted to studs.

With furniture, the main consideration is weight. Well-constructed floors can easily support a tabletop 1½ inches thick or even a little thicker, but for the sake of your floors and your back, you'll probably want to locate the table where it won't have to be moved often.

ABOVE, LEFT: *Made of lightweight concrete, this coffee table includes built-in magazine storage. Concrete can also be used for tabletops, desks, and even game tables.*

ABOVE, RIGHT: *Curved panels of colored concrete, separated by bands of metal trim, create a stunning backdrop for a woodstove.*

LEFT: *Modern fireplaces are often set flush with the wall or are indented only slightly. A fireplace surround creates a greater sense of depth, especially if it incorporates three-dimensional features, such as the angled lines in this design.*

OPPOSITE, BOTTOM LEFT: *Looking like miniature bull's-eyes, glass beads draw stares to this terrazzo-style concrete tabletop.*

OPPOSITE, BOTTOM RIGHT: *A concrete radiator cover formed with a reservoir on top turns a utilitarian fixture into a focal point and adds welcome humidity.*

A concrete fireplace warms up this bedroom. Instead of a traditional hearth, there's a thick ledge hovering above the floor that can be used for sitting.

USING CONCRETE OUTDOORS

Though decorative concrete is still relatively rare as an indoor finish material, it's been used outdoors for decades. Driveways, paths, patios, planter boxes, barbecue areas, and sculptures are just some of the possibilities.

Concrete paving is often poured as a large slab, but it can also be set as individual pavers, much like brick or tile. Besides choosing which look you prefer, also consider practical matters. For a slab, you'll probably need to have the concrete delivered by a mixing truck, so access is important. But once the forms are ready, your project will probably be done in a day. With pavers, it's just the opposite. If you make the pieces yourself, you can mix small batches of concrete and cast one or two pavers at a time. You can carry or wheel pieces to where they are needed, then set them in stages. If you change your mind about the design, simply reuse the pieces in a different place or configuration. With a concrete slab, you'll never need to worry about weeds working their way through the pavement, except perhaps at joints. With pavers, consider filling the joints with grout or using them as miniature planting spaces.

ABOVE: *A concrete countertop is a great choice for an outdoor kitchen. A simple counter might be a project worth tackling yourself, especially if you are worried about attempting one indoors. This version features dark-tinted concrete studded with small glass tiles (inset).*

BELOW: *Concrete can be used to build many projects that might traditionally have been carved from stone, such as an address monument. Make recessed letters like these by placing three-dimensional numbers in a mold.*

ABOVE, LEFT: *This path was poured as a large slab but resembles individual stone tiles. Companies that specialize in this kind of paving typically pour standard gray concrete or a pigmented mix. While the concrete is still slightly flexible, they sprinkle a mixture of cement and pigment (sometimes in several colors) over the top, then press in the texture and grout lines with special mats, rollers, stamps, or other tools. Installers sometimes cut the grout lines with saws or grinders.*

ABOVE, RIGHT: *Outdoor countertops can have all the fancy features you might find in high-end kitchen counters. This version includes a built-in drainage area decorated with brass inlays and a stone insert. The center area was ground down with diamond abrasives, revealing the small stones and sand that went into the concrete mix.*

RIGHT: *Set in a diagonal pattern, pavers make a striking design. Pebbles set into the surface add interest, reduce glare, and help keep the concrete from becoming slippery.*

PUSHING THE LIMITS OF CONCRETE

Because concrete is such a versatile and important building material, researchers are constantly working to develop mixes with better properties. Manufacturers and entrepreneurs, in turn, are busy inventing new ways to use older formulas. They are also experimenting with new ones, such as flexible concrete, see-through concrete, stainproof concrete, and concrete that lights up.

ABOVE: *Bronze pigment makes this concrete sink sparkle as if it were made of metal. The manufacturer, Stone Soup Concrete, mixed the mica-based pigment into the concrete, then polished it with a 1500-grit abrasive to expose particles near the surface.*

LEFT: *Light passes through this concrete when optical glass fibers are incorporated into the mix. Light-transmitting concrete was invented by a Hungarian architect, Aron Losonczi, and is being marketed as Litracon™. The first application suitable for use in houses is a table lamp (far left). There could also be architectural applications (immediate left).*

OPPOSITE, BOTTOM LEFT: *Beneath the colorful plastic coating, this chair is concrete. The 8.0 chair by designer Omer Arbel was cast in one piece without any reinforcement, a feat possible only because it uses a new type of flexible cement known as Ductal®. The manufacturer, Lafarge North America, says Ductal® produces concrete 10 times as strong as usual, which allows it to be used almost as if it were metal.*

Fiber optics in concrete

When concrete is embedded with fiber-optic strands, countertops or other objects light up from within. This constellation design began in an upside-down mold elevated on spacers over a worktable. For each point of light, LifeTime Floors, LLC, drilled a 1/16-inch hole and threaded through a 1 mm-thick fiber-optic strand long enough to reach the light source. Under the mold, the crew bent the end of each strand into a 90-degree angle to keep it from pulling through. Over the mold, the crew taped the long ends of the strands into bundles and pulled them taut as the concrete was added. LifeTime Floors' concrete mix (see page 56) works well for this because it flows easily around the fibers and levels itself. With fibers rising from the surface, it couldn't be troweled. Once the concrete set, the makers flipped the countertop onto spacers (to protect the fibers), scraped the bent fiber ends from the back, and lifted off the mold. Then they polished the surface, connected the light, and—voila!—stars appeared.

ABOVE AND INSET: *The wavy divider, sliding drain tray, and chip-resistant metal inlays in the bottom of the bowls may seem the most striking details of this sink. But it has one feature that's not so obvious: The sink is cast from a type of concrete that the manufacturer, Sonoma Cast Stone, considers stainproof. To bolster the claim, the company sends out "mess kits" and invites recipients to pour red wine, lemon juice, hot sauce, olive oil, and ketchup on samples of the company's standard, sealed concrete, and the stainproof type, known as NuCrete™. The next day, the differences are striking (insets). Standard sealed countertops do resist stains, but if spills are left in place for hours, damage can still occur.*

19

Is concrete right for you?

CHOOSING THE RIGHT MATERIAL for new countertops, sinks, fireplace surrounds, and many other details of a house can be a daunting task. There are so many factors, including price, style, versatility, and performance. In the end, though, the equation often winds up involving a big dose of emotion as well. It makes sense to choose materials that you love.

PRICE

When you buy concrete by the bag at a home center, it seems cheap—less than $5 to make a 1½-inch-thick slab 2 by 2 feet. So it surprises many people that concrete countertops often

cost about $100 a square foot. Part of the difference is that top-rate countertops aren't made with the cheapest concrete mixes, which work fine for setting postholes but aren't up to delivering the crisp details that most people want in a countertop. But the main reason is that materials aren't the biggest cost. Embedded in the price of the professional job are a whole host of tasks: making templates, figuring out spacing for faucets, planning for a way to mount a sink or a cooktop, fabricating molds, ensuring consistent results from one project to the next, polishing and sealing the surface, and transporting and installing the countertop. Many of the tasks are the same as those involved in fabricating and installing first-rate stone countertops, so the prices tend to be similar. Of course, if you're willing to take on the related tasks, you can build your own concrete projects quite inexpensively. The projects in this book are a great way to start.

STYLE

Decorative concrete tugs at the spirits of many people for a variety of reasons. Depending on how you shape and finish the concrete, it can be rough and industrial looking or as finely crafted as elegant china. For some, this freedom with design can be a bit bewildering. It may help to recognize that built-in elements, such as countertops and fireplace surrounds, often look best if they are tailored to the style of the house. Intricate moldings work in a Victorian. In a Craftsman-style home, simpler shapes look best, though you can add carved or molded designs typical of the period. In a contemporary house, you might choose crisp edges and massive shapes.

The variety of fireplace designs shown on these pages illustrates the way concrete can adapt to a wide range of decorating styles.

Oversized corbels and a thick mantel create a style that would work well in a Mission or European country home.

Inset tiles featuring two small rabbits enliven an otherwise simple concrete fireplace surround, in a style that suits Craftsman and other traditional homes.

Cast concrete tinted olive gray serves as a focal point in a contemporary family room. The concrete hearth extends the width of the room and serves as a window seat along the wall to the right.

Concrete tiles with veins of contrasting color hint of marble and give this room an Asian look, especially when paired with an airy flower arrangement.

Mitered corners help this fireplace surround focus attention on the fire, similar to the way a picture frame sets off artwork. The clean lines of the surround also help establish a crisp, modern tone for the room.

VERSATILITY

Concrete is easy to customize, so you can get just the color, size, and shape you want. Whether you form it yourself or hire a pro, you can take advantage of concrete's properties to accomplish things that would be far more difficult with other materials.

❖ It can be mixed where you need it from materials you can carry in manageable loads. For example, you can build massive steps up a hillside without using heavy equipment.

❖ It stiffens on its own. You can use it to make tiles, pots, and other clay-like projects, but you don't need a kiln.

❖ If you time it right, decorative concrete can be carved with little effort and no dust. You can make objects that look like carved stone using only a kitchen knife.

PERFORMANCE

Concrete is as hard and durable as many natural stones. Like some of them, it is porous, so it stains and may crack as it freezes and thaws outdoors. Concrete is also prone to cracking if too much water is used when it is made or if it isn't reinforced properly. All of these problems, though, can be kept to a minimum if you follow the procedures recommended in this book.

One aspect of concrete that people tend to forget is that the surface and the interior often look quite different. A troweled or molded surface looks uniform, while the interior is a jumble of sand, gravel, and cement. So if the surface wears away under heavy traffic, the look will change, though the concrete will remain strong and just as serviceable.

Another thing people tend to forget is that concrete is heavy—about 140 pounds per cubic foot. Countertops 1½ inches thick are not usually a problem, but if you have an older house, you may need to strengthen the floor supports if you add thick countertops in the center of a room. Bathtubs are even more of an issue (see page 10).

Heavy machinery would be needed to place boulders this size. But a homeowner built these steps himself from concrete he mixed in batches in a wheelbarrow and shaped by hand. He scattered pigments onto the surface and troweled them in, creating a variegated appearance similar to that of native stone in the area.

PRECAST OR CAST IN PLACE?

You'll need to decide whether the concrete should be precast (made in a shop or your yard) or formed where you want the finished piece to sit. You may have no choice if access to the spot is so difficult that there would be no way to carry a finished piece to its resting place. But in other situations, there are pros and cons to consider. Precasting keeps the construction mess out of your house. You can inspect the pieces before they are installed and replace any if necessary—an option not possible with a poured-in-place project unless you're willing to undertake a substantial demolition job. Also, because precast objects are usually formed in a mold, you're likely to get uniform, crisp details on edges or other features.

For a project like this, precast concrete is the only way to go. While it's possible to form a rough-looking sink with a trowel, one with sharp angles like these needs to be cast upside down in a mold.

When large projects are cast off site, seams are inevitable. Good design and inspired mold-making turn them into decorative elements.

However, even where access is easy, there is a limit to the size and weight people can carry. Precast countertops usually consist of pieces no more than 7 feet long. Past that, a poured-in-place countertop is your best option. There is no need to make a template for a poured-in-place project—an advantage if you do the work yourself, because it eliminates the risk that you'll accidentally cast a piece upside down or backward. Poured-in-place objects also tend to have more of a handmade appearance because the top surface and sometimes the edge details are formed with a trowel.

Doing it yourself versus hiring a pro

Building your own concrete projects can be fun. But if a mix begins to harden before it's shaped, the process becomes a nightmare. If you're a novice, you may want to focus on garden projects and hire a pro for big indoor jobs. If you do tackle a countertop or other large project, practice on smaller pieces. Get help. And design poured-in-place objects so they can be removed if necessary.

With ingenuity and money, many things become possible. Before this piece was cast, the template makers carefully measured the diagonal distance across the window and adjusted that to leave room for the thickness of the counter. On moving day, the builders brought in a crane to do the heavy lifting.

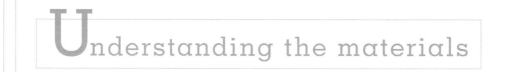

Understanding the materials

MANY PEOPLE USE THE TERMS "cement" and "concrete" interchangeably, but the two materials are not the same. Cement is just glue. Concrete is what you get by mixing cement with aggregate (usually small rocks and sand) and enough water to produce a workable consistency. Some mixes also incorporate fibers, latex or acrylic fortifiers, and other additives.

By tinkering with the ingredients and ways of shaping concrete, you can get just the look you want. For example, you can choose between standard gray cement or cement that is nearly pure white, a decision that will affect the way pigment tints the concrete. You also have a choice of which sand or gravel to use. Depending on the finish of the piece, this may or may not make a big difference in the final appearance. And you have a wide range of options for adding color.

The following pages explore each of the variables in more detail. The effects shown here may point you to the look you want for your own home.

ABOVE: *To create the contrasting colors in this driveway-turned-basketball court, the builder framed and poured the red areas, then removed the forms and poured the tan expanses. Because the pigment was added to the other ingredients, it will never wear off.*

BELOW: *The swirling colors in this floor were created with acid stains, which react with ingredients in the concrete to produce colors that differ slightly from one area to the next. Two colors of stain were used here.*

ABOVE, LEFT: *This stool has a marbleized look because of how it was made. First rose-colored concrete was pressed into a mold one handful at a time. After the mold was removed, gaps between those handfuls were filled with buff-colored concrete.*

ABOVE, RIGHT: *Placing a slick form liner into a mold created the shiny, somewhat wrinkled-looking surface on this countertop. Note the "hospital bed" corner. See page 94 for tips on creating a similar look with plastic as a mold liner.*

RIGHT: *This countertop illustrates the range of decorative options you have with concrete. The countertop was first cast from red-tinted concrete. Grinding one end revealed an agate inlay as well as the mixture of sand particles that went into the concrete. The rest of the counter was left with its surface skin intact, and the color was enhanced with acid stains.*

WATER

In examining the ingredients that go into concrete, it may seem strange to look at water first. But it's actually the key to how concrete projects turn out. Water makes concrete easy to shape, and it sets off a chemical reaction known as hydration that causes the cement to harden. But if there is too much water, the structure will become weak and prone to cracking. The excess water goes to the surface as the concrete is troweled, creating tiny tunnels that remain when the mix hardens. The tunnels make concrete porous, which leads to staining and frost damage.

Concrete made with white cement, not the usual gray, produces vibrant color like that in this bathroom. Concrete tiles on the walls, the steps, and the base of the tub surround were custom-colored to complement marble around the top of the tub and the tumbled marble tiles on the floor.

6% AIR

11% PORTLAND CEMENT

41% GRAVEL OR CRUSHED STONE (COARSE AGGREGATE)

26% SAND (FINE AGGREGATE)

16% WATER

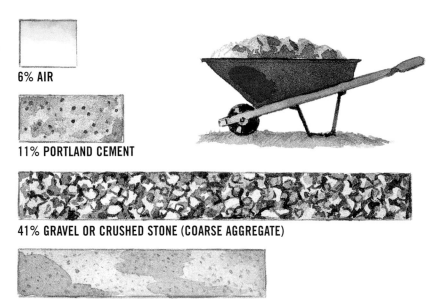

Although it's the key to holding everything together, cement accounts for the least bulk of all the major ingredients in concrete. There are many recipes for concrete, so proportions vary.

CEMENT

The most common cement, known as portland cement, comes in a variety of types, but for decorative projects the main choice involves two options: white or gray. White cement costs more and is harder to find in some areas. But it's worth considering, as it allows pigments to produce bright colors. Tinting gray cement produces muted colors.

Small amounts of specialty cements, such as fly ash or metakaolin, are often incorporated in mixes used for countertops, sinks, and other decorative pieces. Known as pozzolans, these fine powders act like miniature BBs, helping other ingredients slip into place with less water. This results in a denser, stronger concrete with crisp details.

How cement color affects tints

Each pair of color samples below shows how an identical amount of pigment tints white and gray cement.

On the other hand, once cement stiffens, abundant moisture is good. It allows hydration to continue, so the concrete becomes even harder and more crack resistant. Once the concrete dries, however, hydration ceases. Adding water after that point won't restart the process.

AGGREGATE

Sand and gravel play two roles in the projects presented in this book: structural and decorative. From a structural standpoint, sand and especially gravel are what give concrete its strength. They, not cement, should account for most of the volume. A range of particle sizes works best because it allows small pieces to fit between big ones. However, the biggest particles should not exceed one-fifth the thickness of a structure, or the concrete may break apart.

Many countertop manufacturers omit gravel when they pour slabs up to 2 inches thick. Instead of gravel, these companies often rely on metal or fiber reinforcement to make the concrete strong and to keep it crack-free.

To learn about decorative aggregate, see pages 34–35.

WHITE CEMENT   GRAY CEMENT

TINTING CONCRETE WITH PIGMENT

There are many ways to color concrete, but the most common method calls for adding pigment to the other ingredients at the time the concrete is mixed. These pigments must be able to stand up to the alkalinity of cement. If the concrete will be outdoors, the pigments must also resist fading when exposed to ultraviolet light from the sun. Iron oxides perform well in both ways, so it's no surprise that many pigment colors are based on them. Everyone is familiar with the most common kind of iron oxide: rust. It's what makes soil red in some parts of the country. Yellow, another form of iron oxide, results when small amounts of other minerals are present. When these natural deposits or their synthetic equivalents are prepared and sold as artists' pigments, labels may say "ochre," "umber," or "burnt sienna."

Many concrete colorants are based on mineral pigments, and the resulting colors are mostly earth tones. On the samples shelf at one manufacturer, it would be hard to find two colors that clash.

Practical and environmental concerns

Incorporating pigment as you mix concrete is the quickest, most foolproof way to add color. There's no extra labor, and you wind up with a mixture that's tinted all the way through. If any edges on the finished product chip, the newly exposed concrete will blend in.

The best color for a project is more than just a matter of style. Red, yellow, and brown pigments resist fading best, an important consideration if you are using concrete outdoors. Blue pigment darkens and black pigment fades over time in sunlight, so the color won't stay as intense. Green and blue pigments are usually based on copper, cobalt, or chromium. These are heavy metals that are extremely toxic to aquatic life, so working with such pigments requires extra care (see page 51). If you live near a stream or lake, you may wish to avoid using these colors on outdoor projects, where rinse water or erosion might carry bits of pigment into the water. Red, yellow, and brown pigments are environmentally benign and cheaper than the greens and blues.

Color matching

Professionals need to produce finished pieces that match their color samples, so they either weigh ingredients carefully or buy pigment pre-measured to tint a specific amount of concrete. This is the best way to ensure consistency from batch to batch. A difference in any ingredient, including water, will affect the final result. Even with accurate measuring, however, color differences can still result because of changes in temperature, troweling, and the time needed to place the concrete. Instead of fretting about slight variations, celebrate them as hallmarks of a handmade product.

Color intensity

When you select a color for your project, you can choose a light tint or a more saturated hue. But there is a limit to how deep the color can get—and it's never even close to the brilliance of pure pigment. Once pigment totals about 10 percent of the cement, or even less, the color is usually as intense as it will get. Coincidentally, 10 percent is also the point at which adding more pigment begins to weaken concrete.

These samples show how varying the amount of one blue pigment affects the color of concrete mixed with white cement. With gray cement or some pigments, color differences may be less pronounced.

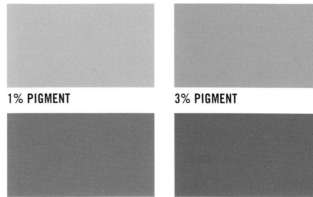

1% PIGMENT   **3% PIGMENT**

7% PIGMENT   **10% PIGMENT**

Creative options

If you are building your own projects, you might want to experiment with different ways of adding color, especially if you have leftover ingredients from other jobs. Besides incorporating pigments and stains sold specifically for concrete, you may be able to use powdered pigments sold in some paint stores. If the pigments are iron oxides or are labeled with terms such as "umber" or "ochre," they should work fine. Wood stains may also work. You can even tint concrete by substituting water-based paint for some or all of the water that you'd normally use. It's a way to use up leftover paint, especially on small projects. If you are not sure whether a colorant will work, leave a sample outdoors for a month to see whether it fades noticeably.

RIGHT: *To create this patio, the builder began by pouring concrete that was lightly tinted with a buff pigment. He then rolled out a paper stencil to create the look of grout lines and broadcast a slightly different tone of color hardener over it. He used a textured roller to create the rippled surface.*

SPREADING PIGMENT ON THE SURFACE

Dry pigment can also be sprinkled over the surface and troweled in as the concrete hardens. Commercial products designed for this use are sold as "color hardener" or "dry shake." They consist mostly of dry pigment, cement, and fine sand. There is no additional water, just the excess moisture on the surface of the concrete. This approach creates a harder surface that's more wear resistant. It also saves money because it uses less pigment. And because several colors can be sprinkled on randomly, it results in rich color variations.

Broadcast pigments are often used in combination with textured rollers, stamps, or mats to simulate the look of brick or stone paving. The mixture of pigment, cement, and sand keeps the texturing tools from sticking to the concrete.

LEFT: *Several tones of color hardener broadcast onto freshly poured concrete created the varied shades in this path. The grout lines look realistic because they were cut out with a grinder and filled with mortar. The mortar is shallow and has solid concrete underneath, so there is less chance that weeds will grow in the joints.*

Overview

Acid stains can produce vivid or very muted effects, depending on how they're used. A light touch prevails on this bar sink and backsplash. The simple band of red stain on the counter emphasizes the curve of the bowl.

COLORING CONCRETE WITH ACID STAINS

Acid stains are alchemist tools for coloring concrete. You don't know what they will look like until the job is done.

These stains consist of acidic solutions rich with metallic salts. When they're brushed, sprayed, or rubbed onto concrete, they may look almost clear. The acid etches the surface, allowing the salts to react with hydrated lime in the hardened concrete. This results in colored compounds permanently bonded to the surface. Each job and even different parts of the same job usually turn out a little different because the final color depends on the aggregate incorporated, the additives used when the concrete was poured, the tools and techniques used to smooth the concrete, as well as many other factors.

Stains come in shades of black, brown, rusty red, gold, and blue-green (as shown at right). Some manufacturers warn that per-

sistent moisture might darken some colors, particularly blue-green. Use these stains in indoor areas where the concrete will stay dry.

Custom colors and effects

Acid stains are available in only a few stock colors, but they can be used to create many effects. Diluting a stain before it's applied softens the shade. Applying multiple coats darkens the color and evens out areas where the first coat did not penetrate well or where brushstrokes show.

Acid stains can also create designs of several distinct colors. Outlining the design by first cutting a shallow groove in the concrete keeps colors from bleeding into each other. After the staining is complete, the grooves can be left or filled with grout. Manufacturers also make acid-resistant gels for outlining areas. These products peel up once the stains are set. Tape and stencils are other options.

Acid stains, painted in overlapping bands over gray concrete, give this countertop and backsplash a vividly colored look reminiscent of a wood burl or a geode.

Other concrete stains

Although acid stains get the most attention, manufacturers also make water-based and solvent-based stains. Just as wood stains only partially mask the natural patterns in wood, these stains allow some of the natural variations in concrete to show. The water-based formulas contain acrylic resins, just as most water-based paints do. But unlike paint, which is prone to peeling if moisture moves through the concrete, these stains still allow moisture to pass through. The solvent-based formulas use mostly acetone to carry the color into the concrete. This solvent, most commonly recognized as fingernail polish remover, doesn't contribute to smog formation, so it can still be sold even where other solvents are highly restricted. Acetone is very flammable, however, so any nearby flames must be extinguished before it is used.

For colors not possible with acid dyes, such as deep blue and bright yellow, concrete artisans turn to water-based dyes.

APPLYING DECORATIVE TOPPINGS

Thin cement-based coatings are another way to create decorative effects on concrete. These products mask damaged concrete and thus provide a fresh canvas. They are also used on new concrete because they can be applied near the end of a construction project, when there is less chance of damage and more time for artistic effects that might be too complex to undertake when the floor is being poured. Toppings can cover concrete blocks, poured concrete walls, old laminate countertops, drywall, and many other surfaces.

ABOVE: *Concrete overlays can be decorated with the full range of techniques that work on regular concrete. A look like this results from acid stains and decorative saw cuts.*

BELOW, LEFT: *Yellow and red acid stains applied in a random, overlapping manner create the lively look on this floor. Acid stains are often applied to poured-in-place concrete floors, allowing the subfloor to double as the finished floor surface. However, if the slab is old or scuffed up, it works better to coat the concrete base with a concrete topping mix and then apply the acid stain to that fresh, smooth surface.*

BELOW, RIGHT: *To create intricate designs in which each color remains distinct, installers often tape off adjoining sections before they apply stain, much as decorative painters do when they paint stripes on a wall. For even crisper lines, they sometimes outline sections by cutting grooves into the concrete with a concrete saw or a grinder.*

ABOVE: *The concrete shelves, counter, and cabinets in this kitchen were created with a gray cement-based overlay. The supports for the counter are concrete blocks, which the builder covered with metal lath and then the overlay. He built the shelves and counter of wood and then covered that with the lath and overlay.*

These products go by various names: concrete overlays, polymer refinishing systems, and micro toppings. They contain cement, polymers, sand, and sometimes pebbles. Some coatings are designed to be 2 or 3 inches thick, while others add just $1/16$ inch. Though thicker coatings look just like concrete when they cure, some extremely thin overlays depend on such fine sand and so much polymer that they end up resembling plastic more than concrete.

The overlays allow for all of the standard ways of coloring concrete: mixing in pigment, coloring the surface with stains, and cutting decorative lines. In addition, some products can be colored with a full rainbow of brilliant colors, not just the earth tones usually associated with concrete pigments and stains.

TOPPING CONCRETE WITH PAINT

Plain old paint also works on concrete. Just avoid using it where moisture might wick through the concrete, such as on a basement floor. Paint there is likely to peel. Over new concrete, wait to apply oil-based stains or paints until the concrete is thoroughly dry—at least a month old. With water-based finishes, the timing isn't as critical.

Tip

OVERLAYS WORK WON-DERFULLY to create a fresh look on concrete with dings and gouges. But if the concrete has cracks caused by uneven settling of the ground, don't count on an overlay to make them disappear. The underlying cracks will continue to open up and will eventually show in the overlay. Instead of trying to mask the cracks, fill them with polyurethane joint sealant. If you then apply a topping over that, make the path of the crack part of the design (see page 91).

Paint dresses up this concrete patio and makes the floor easier to wipe clean.

USING AGGREGATE AS DECORATION

Concrete always contains aggregate—sand and usually gravel. But a thin film of cement forms along the surface, so the aggregate in most projects remains submerged. It takes extra steps to give it a decorative role.

There are two basic approaches: scatter additional aggregate on the surface and embed it at least partway while the concrete is still workable, or wear away the surface cement to reveal the aggregate mixed into the interior. Sprinkling aggregate on top tends to leave the surface rougher than it would be if it were polished. This could be an advantage or a disadvantage, depending on your situation. Another consideration is cost. If you want an expensive aggregate, such as mother-of-pearl, you'll see more of what you pay for if you broadcast it onto the surface rather than use it all the way through. But incorporating the decorative aggregate into the mix reduces the risk that some of the particles will pop out. A good compromise may be mixing the decorative material into only the concrete that will be near the surface.

TOP: *Flecks of recycled glass catch light and reflect it in different directions, giving this countertop a translucent quality even though it is actually opaque.*

ABOVE: *Grinding only the edges of a piece results in an entirely different look.*

WHITE MARBLE DUST

BLACK PEBBLE SAND

SILICA SAND

TAN SAND

GRANITE SAND

GRANUSIL BLASTING SAND

BLACK PEBBLES

MOTHER-OF-PEARL

ROSE MARBLE

When contractors who specialize in outdoor pavement talk about exposed aggregate, they're referring to a pebbly surface like this. Contrasting bands of brick dress up its look.

Using glass aggregate

You may be tempted to use broken glass for some or all of the aggregate. However, researchers who study industrial uses of concrete have found that some glass reacts with the alkaline content of cement when moisture is present for long periods. An expansive gel forms at the glass edges, cracking the concrete or ejecting some of the surface glass. In something like a dam, for example, this phenomenon is a critical issue. In decorative home projects, however, it's less of a problem. For outdoor applications, take the precaution of replacing part of the mix water with acrylic or latex fortifier. This substance looks like thin white glue and may be labeled as concrete bonding adhesive. Also consider switching to white cement, which has a low alkaline content. Adding metakaolin also helps prevent the problem. Indoors, there is no concern except on a shower floor or in a sink.

BLACK AND WHITE MARBLE

GREEN MARBLE

ROAN RIVER PEBBLES

BUCKSKIN QUARTZ

CREAM STONE

PEA GRAVEL

TUMBLED RECYCLED GLASS

STAINED-GLASS SHARDS

COBALT-BLUE TUMBLED GLASS

Overview

GETTING CREATIVE WITH INLAYS

Inlays are the jewelry of decorative concrete. Like necklaces, they range from flashy to understated, and they often evoke personal memories. Many manufacturers, recognizing how much people value personal touches in their homes, invite customers to select and even place inlays in their countertops or fireplace surrounds. Of course, if you are creating your own concrete projects, you can do this without any invitation.

There are only a few basic caveats:

❖ Avoid using items made from aluminum, as this metal can't stand up to the high alkalinity of cement.

❖ In most cases, choose inlays that are no more than one-fifth the thickness of the counter, the same rule you'd use in selecting aggregate.

❖ Avoid inlays that are extremely thin, as they can pop out.

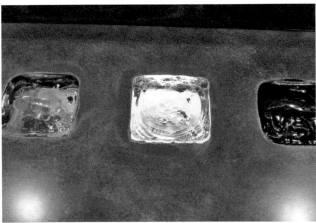

ABOVE: *The owner of this countertop collects coins from around the world. Now he gets to look at some of them every day.*

RIGHT: *An ammonite fossil makes a stunning inlay.*

OPPOSITE, MIDDLE: *Glass inlays in this countertop extend all the way through the concrete, allowing light to shine through from a fixture underneath.*

OPPOSITE, BOTTOM: *Bits of tile create a sunburst design in this countertop.*

CHOOSING SURFACE TEXTURE

In look and feel, there's a big difference between a diamond-polished countertop and most patio paving. One needs to be slick so spills wipe up easily, while the other must be rough enough to keep people from slipping, even in the rain. Luckily, concrete can wear many coats, from slick to rough. The finish you choose plays a big role in the overall appearance of your project.

Basic options

These four samples all consist of identical proportions of cement, pigment, sand, and other ingredients. But up close, the surfaces look quite different. If you could touch them, you'd notice that their textures range from smooth to rough.

ABOVE: *All of this concrete started out looking the same. But installers coated the edge bands with a solution that keeps cement from hardening, and they later rinsed those areas with a power washer. This removed the skim surface of cement and fine sand and exposed gravel within the concrete mix, creating the decorative, two-tone look. The rest of the concrete has a broom finish, made by brushing across the concrete before it is fully hardened. This finish adds texture, which makes the concrete slip-resistant.*

Straight from the mold and not sanded or sealed, this surface is smooth but not slippery. The color is slightly mottled and the surface is matte.

For this satin-smooth finish, the air holes were filled with cement slurry. The surface was polished with diamond abrasives, then sealed and waxed.

Washed with an acid etch, this surface is rougher. Because it has lost its skin of cement, pigment, and fine sand, you can see the sand particles in the mix. Sanding the surface with diamond abrasives would have created a similar look with a smooth surface.

A more powerful acid etching gave this sample a rougher texture. Air holes were left unfilled, which gives the piece a more rustic look.

RIGHT: *Textured and tinted to resemble stone, this concrete patio pairs well with the neo-classical fountain at the center. The texture also creates a more slip-resistant surface.*

ABOVE: *This concrete with a salt finish was troweled smooth, then sprinkled with rock salt. Where the salt landed, the cement didn't cure properly and holes formed. Because the texture adds slip resistance, it's great near pools and on walkways. But the pockets trap water, so this finish is not a good choice where temperatures frequently drop below freezing. Because water expands as it becomes ice, the concrete would break down.*

LEFT: *Sometimes a hands-off approach to finishing works best. This countertop, cast upside down in a mold, has its brilliant monochrome color partly because it was left with its molded surface intact. The pigment was mixed into the concrete, then placed in the mold, where fine pigment, cement, and superfine sand settled on the bottom (now the top of the countertop). Grinding that surface with fine abrasives would have removed some of the highly colored film, causing the aggregate color to influence the overall look. Because pigment colors only the cement, not the aggregate, the color would not be as intense.*

39

Working with concrete

THE FOLLOWING PAGES discuss the basics of molding and shaping concrete, how to prevent cracks, and how to trowel and finish a job. They focus on casting concrete into a mold— a technique you can use to build everything from simple steppingstones or tabletops to complex countertops, fireplace surrounds, and walkways. You'll also find information about lesser-known techniques, including carving concrete and sculpting it into three-dimensional pieces, such as garden art.

CASTING ON THE GROUND

When you cast concrete for a walkway, patio, or decorative edging strip, you don't need to worry about making the base perfectly level. The top edge of the forms is the critical feature.

Mark the perimeter with string or spray paint. Without disturbing underlying soil, dig straight down at least 2 inches for small projects such as steppingstones. Cast small objects directly on soil. For patios and paths, dig at least 6 inches down to allow a slightly elevated 4-inch slab (minimum thickness) over a 4-inch bed of crushed rock or pea gravel. Adding gravel to the hole before you build the form is easier than shoveling gravel in later.

PLANNING INDOOR PROJECTS

Countertops and other indoor projects may be built in place or precast, which means they are molded in a workshop or garage and then moved into place. Precasting is most common because it keeps the mess out of the house and makes it easier to redo projects if they don't turn out right.

Setting up a good workspace is very important. Although it's possible to build concrete projects outside, work indoors whenever possible so you don't have to battle wind and sun, which make concrete stiffen faster.

Two layers of benderboard (or use ¼-inch plywood)

Stakes every 3 feet or less; trim flush

2 by 4 set on edge

Slope of at least ⅛ inch per foot so water runs off

Dirt, gravel, or strips of wood to keep concrete from oozing out

| Melamine-coated particleboard | Details in reverse | ¾-inch plywood base | 2 by 4s on edge to prevent sagging | Homemade brace |

HOME SETUP

In a home workshop, you can create a sturdy worktable supported by sawhorses and 2 by 4s, but don't skimp on the support structure. For a 4-by-8-foot table, set up two sawhorses near each end plus one in the middle. Top those with four or more evenly spaced 8-foot-long 2 by 4s set on edge so they resist sagging. Screw a sheet of plywood to the 2 by 4s so nothing shifts. Top that with whatever you are using for the bottom of your mold. Check the table with a level. If it's not right, work shims under the sawhorses or the 2 by 4s.

Mold options

To mold a tabletop, counter, or other flat object, you can work either right side up and shape the top surface by hand, or right side down and let the mold do the smoothing. With a right-side-up project, what you see is what you get. If your pour will be facedown, you will need to build every detail of the mold in reverse. For numbers, letters, or other features whose orientation matters, make the mold a mirror image of what you want.

There are two basic ways to build a mold for a tabletop or other slab. You can screw sidepieces onto an oversize bottom piece that doubles as the top surface of your worktable. Or you can cut a base piece the same size as your project and then screw sidepieces to that. If you take the latter approach, just be sure to cut the sides ¾ inch deeper so they fit around a ¾-inch-thick base. If you don't screw the sides to the tabletop, add braces (see picture above) so the sides don't bow out from the pressure of the concrete.

Mold materials

Most concrete artists build molds from ¾-inch-thick particleboard coated with melamine, a plastic that doesn't stick to concrete. Home centers and lumberyards sell it in 4-by-8-foot sheets as well as in smaller sizes for shelving. For more complex shapes, such as sink knockouts, use foam insulation board (with double-stick tape to build up layers, if necessary) or polystyrene foam (Styrofoam). Cut these materials with a knife or saw, then shape them with a rasp. Smooth them with drywall mud or cover the edges with plastic tape or mason's polyethylene tape.

UNDERSTANDING CRACKS AND HOW TO PREVENT THEM

Some concrete objects need metal or fiber reinforcement to keep them from cracking. Others do fine without it. Understanding why concrete cracks and how reinforcement works will help you decide when to add it. When in doubt, put it in. Reinforcement is cheap insurance.

Cracks caused by excess water

Concrete often develops small surface cracks that are caused by excess water in the mix. Adding thin fibers reduces or eliminates this problem, as does limiting the water you add. You can substitute acrylic or latex fortifier (sometimes labeled as concrete bonding adhe-sive) for some of the water. Or add specialty cements, such as metakaolin, or switch to a concrete mix that incorporates them.

Cracks caused by lack of stiffness

Concrete doesn't crush easily, but it has little ability to withstand bending or stretching. Reinforcement adds the strength it lacks on its own. To decide whether you need to add it, consider what stresses will be on the concrete. A path on undisturbed ground where erosion isn't likely is probably fine without it. But reinforcement would help on a countertop with an overhang, a garden bench that spans several feet, or a precast countertop that you may knock while moving. Options include metal reinforcement, glass fibers, and a carbon-fiber grid. Flexible fibers also add stiffness, though not as much.

Cracks caused by shrinkage

As concrete cures, it slowly shrinks because it is losing water. Concrete made with a minimum of water cracks least. You can also minimize cracks by adding joints or cutting grooves in the hardening concrete. These give it a way to shrink without cracking in other places. To determine where these spaces need to be, multiply the slab's thickness in inches by $2\frac{1}{2}$. The result is the maximum number of feet that should be in a section. For example, a pathway 4 inches thick requires a break every 10 feet.

Even with enough joints, long, skinny rectangles and interior corners on L-shaped objects still often crack because the ends don't shrink together. Avoid problems by redesigning your project into squares and short rectangles, if possible. If you can't avoid weak shapes, reinforce them to help the concrete move as one piece. Use rebar or welded-wire mesh with gravel-based concrete and welded-wire mesh, expanded-metal lath, or masonry block ladder wire with sand mixes.

One seam resolves several practical issues with the elevated portion of this countertop. If the counter had been cast in one piece, the two sections would have pulled apart slightly as water in the mix evaporated. To relieve that stress, a crack might have opened up at the corner. The seam eliminated that risk. It also made the mold easier to build. And dividing the project into smaller pieces made the countertop easier to move into place.

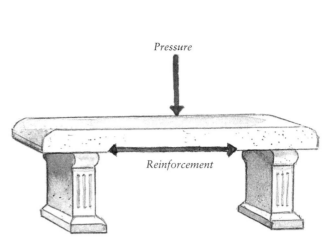

When a concrete bench or other object spans a long distance, the lower side begins to stretch if too much weight is on top. Prevent cracks by placing reinforcement there, toward the bottom of the slab.

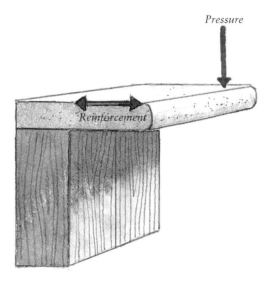

When a counter, hearth, or other object cantilevers, pressing down on the top forces it to stretch. Prevent this by placing the reinforcement toward the top of the slab.

TOP: *Too much water in the initial mix resulted in these surface cracks.*

MIDDLE: *When its support eroded, this concrete cracked from lack of stiffness.*

BOTTOM: *To round a corner, this concrete walkway was cast into an L shape. It cracked at the corner.*

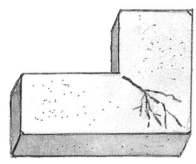

An L-shaped project may crack at the corner.

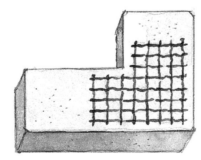

Add reinforcement that spans the corner.

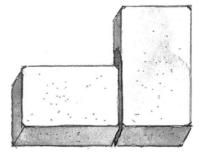

Or divide the project into rectangles.

USING METAL REINFORCEMENT

Adding a few pieces of metal reinforcement may make all the difference in keeping your project intact. But don't expect metal to prevent cracks caused by excessive water or lack of adequate control joints.

Although rebar plays a big role in fortifying structural features built from concrete, it's far less common in decorative projects of the type featured in this book. One reason is that adding rebar to relatively thin slabs can actually cause the concrete to crack. Rebar close to a surface will rust if the concrete absorbs moisture. Rusted rebar pushes on the concrete and breaks it if the concrete is not thick enough, especially if it's made without gravel. In thin pours, rebar can also do what's called ghosting, causing white lines to show on the surface over the metal.

For 1½-inch countertops and similar objects, choose thinner metal reinforcement. There are many options, including mesh types that help knit together the concrete so it expands and contracts as one unit.

You might wonder why metals that do not rust, such as copper or aluminum, aren't used as reinforcement. The Romans, who worked with an early form of cement, discovered when they tried bronze reinforcement that it broke the concrete. We know now that's because bronze, like most other metals, expands and contracts from temperature changes at a different rate than concrete does. Steel, though, moves in step with concrete.

Types

For projects similar to those in this book, your metal-reinforcement choices range from quite stiff to rather flexible (see below).

REBAR AND THREADED ROD

Use ½-inch rods for objects more than 3 inches thick and ⅜-inch rebar for objects about 2½ inches thick. For projects about 1½ inches thick, use threaded rod ¼ inch in diameter. Substitute wire for rebar on even thinner objects.

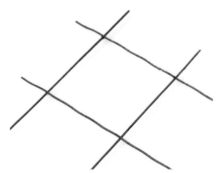

WELDED-WIRE MESH

Also known as remesh. Sold flat in 4-by-7-foot sheets. Get 4-inch or 6-inch openings.

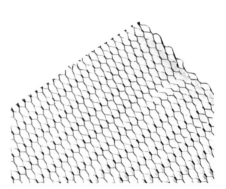

EXPANDED-METAL LATH

Also called diamond mesh. Sold in 27-by-96-inch sheets. The gauge rated at 2.5 pounds per square yard works well with sand mixes. Buy it galvanized.

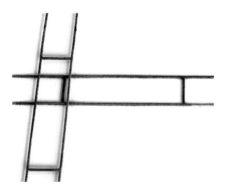

LADDER WIRE

Sold at masonry-supply stores, it consists of a pair of thin rods with welded-on crosspieces, giving it the look of a ladder. It substitutes for rebar on thin objects.

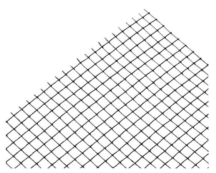

HARDWARE CLOTH

Sold in rolls with openings as small as ¼ inch. Buy it galvanized.

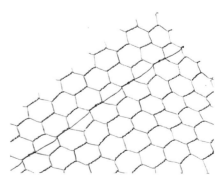

CHICKEN WIRE

For sculptures and free-form projects. Can be bent into complex shapes more easily than hardware cloth. Sold in rolls of various widths, usually with 1-inch openings.

Metal mesh

Originally developed as a backing for stucco, expanded-metal lath is sturdier than some other kinds of metal mesh, including hardware cloth and chicken wire. Metal mesh helps tie concrete together so that it expands and contracts as one unit. It's especially useful in preventing cracks in L-shaped counters or other projects with L shapes, such as the junction of walls and bottoms in sinks.

For any kind of metal mesh to be effective, aggregate in the mix must be small enough to slip through the openings in the metal. Expanded-metal lath works with concrete mixes that have sand-sized aggregate, not gravel.

Metal mesh should stop 1 inch shy of all edges. Cut mesh with tin snips or aviator's snips. Especially with lath, you may want to wear gloves to protect your skin.

Bridge L-shaped sections with a single piece cut to fit, or place a separate piece on each leg and overlap the pieces at the corner. For deeper objects such as sinks, bend the mesh around corners. It's fine to use a different piece of mesh for each corner. Mesh

Cut expanded-metal lath with tin snips or aviator's snips. To keep mesh from cutting you, pull up one side with your free hand. You may also need to hold down the other side with a clamp or your foot.

should go in the middle of the concrete, so it's usually lowered into the mold when about half the concrete is in place.

Expanded-metal lath is sold in sheets 8 feet long and a little over 2 feet wide. Some home centers carry it. If you don't find it there, go to a company that sells stucco or masonry supplies. Hardware cloth and chicken wire are sold in rolls of various widths. Some companies also sell these materials by the foot, so you can buy only as much as you need. If you are forming three-dimensional objects and want simple cone- or column shapes, hardware cloth is the best choice. For more complex shapes, chicken wire works better because you can compress or stretch openings as needed. For more about using metal mesh to create garden ornaments and other sculpture-type pieces, see pages 74–76.

45

Because ladder wire's main purpose is to add strength, thus keeping concrete from bending and cracking, you'll need to set the wire toward the bottom of a slab that will extend between two supports. Set it toward the top in cantilever situations, such as breakfast bars.

Ladder wire

Rebar is too thick for many countertops and other structures, so the decorative-concrete industry borrows reinforcement products from other industries. Ladder wire, which masons use as horizontal reinforcement in concrete-block walls, is one of them. The material consists of 9-gauge wire with welded crosspieces. This ladder-like structure allows the metal to stiffen concrete more effectively than single strands of wire would. A thick, irregular galvanized coating on the ladder wire deters rust and helps concrete grip well. Use bolt cutters to trim ladder wire to size. You can also cut it with a hacksaw.

Rebar

Use rebar primarily to add stiffness to thick concrete that might stretch or bend without it. For example, a garden bench that's supported by posts at both ends might need help to keep from stretching when a lot of weight is applied in the middle. Just be sure to match the reinforcement to the thickness of the object so at least 1 inch of concrete surrounds the metal.

Professionals use special tools for shaping rebar and twisting wire, but for small, occasional projects, you can improvise. Cut rebar with a hacksaw. To join pieces, overlap the ends by at least several inches and lash them tightly with 22-gauge tie wire.

For cast-in-place projects, professionals use premade "chairs" to hold rebar at the proper level. You can bend similar supports from stiff wire or hang the rebar from wire fastened to wooden strips tacked across the top of the form.

Carbon-fiber mesh

Carbon-fiber mesh is the latest innovation in concrete reinforcement. Made from carbon fibers and epoxy, it could be mistaken for a black version of the plastic netting used around some construction sites. You can cut it with scissors, yet it's as effective as steel in stiffening concrete. By weight, it is 8 to 10 times as strong as steel. Because it doesn't rust, carbon-fiber mesh can be placed close to the surface, so it's ideal for reinforcing thin concrete objects.

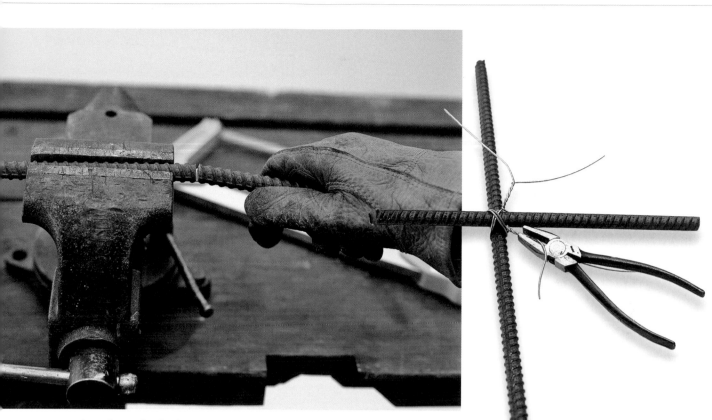

ABOVE: *Cut rebar with a hacksaw, jigsaw, or reciprocating saw. You can stop partway through and snap the waste free.*

RIGHT: *Hold intersecting lengths of rebar together with wire twisted tightly with lineman's pliers. If joints still wobble, wrap them again in a crisscross fashion.*

BELOW: *A long, thick table like this is a good candidate for rebar.*

BELOW: *Carbon-fiber mesh consists of carbon fibers and epoxy formed into a grid. This sample is based on a 1-by-1-inch grid.*

USING FIBER REINFORCEMENT

When you open a bag of fiber reinforcement for the first time, it's hard to believe that something so tiny can do so much. Nylon and polypropylene fibers are whisper thin, flexible, and generally about half an inch long, while glass fibers are stiff, needle-like, and a bit longer. With all kinds of fibers, bundles disperse as the strands are mixed into the concrete along with the other ingredients. Randomly distributed, the fibers help hold concrete together because they straddle areas that might otherwise crack. All types of fibers help protect concrete from fine surface cracks and guard against shrinkage cracks. Glass fibers also add significant stiffness.

Polypropylene fibers

These are the most readily available. Concrete-supply companies sell them in 1-pound bags that disintegrate in a cement mixer. Manufacturers recommend using one or two bags per cubic yard of concrete, so for a single bag of concrete mix you'll need just a few pinches. Using more won't create problems, however. If fibers poke out from the surface once your project is complete, wait for the object to cure, then burn the strands off with a propane torch.

Glass fibers

Glass fibers have the benefits of plastic but also add strength. Products manufactured for use in concrete are alkali resistant, so they won't break down if they come into contact with concrete for long periods. Don't improvise by using chopped strands of fiberglass insulation.

Glass fibers can't be singed off like polypropylene fibers can, so avoid using them near the surface. Be especially careful if you plan to do a lot of grinding to expose an object's aggregate. If sanding unearths glass fibers as well, the surface will have a fuzzy feel. Instead, use concrete free of fibers near the surface and backfill with fiber-enriched concrete.

TOP: *When you want to use polypropylene fibers on something you are casting upside down in a mold, first spread a thin layer of concrete that doesn't have fibers. Cover the entire mold surface, including the sides.*

MIDDLE: *Mix fibers into the remaining concrete. Glass fibers disperse quickly, but plastic ones sometimes clump if you stop mixing too soon.*

BOTTOM: *Fill the rest of the mold with the fiber-rich concrete mix. Because the fiber ends won't be on the surface when the mold is removed, you don't have to worry about singeing them off with a propane torch.*

Tip

BESIDES ADDING FIBERS to bagged mixes or concrete you mix from scratch, you can also buy products with fibers. These include fiber cement mix, which contains gravel and can be used for objects at least 2 inches thick, and surface-bonding cement, designed for thin applications.

This concrete table is an inch thick and 12 feet long, with supports only at the ends—far too thin for that long of a span, according to concrete industry standards. Yet the artisan who made it has stood on it in the middle, and it is still free of cracks. Its secret? The concrete mix includes glass fibers.

Buddy Rhodes, who helped create the concrete countertop industry, started out as a potter but wound up wanting to do projects that were too big for his kiln. Then he discovered concrete, which hardens on its own. Today, when he wants to create giant-size pots like this, he forms the exterior by pressing a thin layer of concrete against a mold that comes apart in sections. To reinforce the concrete, he then mixes polypropylene fibers into the remaining concrete and plasters that over the first layer. He smooths the inside surface of the pot by hand.

ADDING THE CONCRETE

With the mold done and the reinforcement ready, at last it's time to start thinking about adding the concrete. As with food, you can mix up a batch from scratch, use a bagged mix (the equivalent of a just-add-water cake mix), or go the order-in route and arrange for delivery of concrete that's ready to put into a mold.

Ready-to-pour concrete

Standard revolving-barrel mixers usually won't deliver less than 1 cubic yard—enough concrete to pour a 4-inch-thick pad 8 by 10 feet. With concrete, what you order is what you get. The truck won't take leftovers back to the plant. This rules out standard truck delivery for most small projects. However, depending on what's available in your area, you might be able to get smaller amounts of ready-to-pour concrete two other ways: by arranging for a short-pour truck, which carries ingredients in separate bins and mixes them at the job site, or by renting a haul-away trailer from a company that also supplies the mixed concrete.

Mix-it-yourself options

If you want to mix the concrete yourself, weigh the pros and cons of starting from scratch versus using a bagged mix. Unless you need only very small quantities, it's cheaper to mix recipes from scratch than it is to buy bagged mixes. You'll save the most if you order sand and gravel in bulk. However, cement is typically sold only in 94-pound bags, while mixes weigh as little as 40 pounds per bag. If you have a bad back, this advantage might matter more than the cost. Storage is another issue. Bagged mixes need to be kept in a dry area but are fairly compact, while piles of aggregate can be left out in the weather but occupy a lot of space. Some people like mixing from scratch because it allows them to experiment with ingredients. Others appreciate the fact that bagged mixes help ensure consistency from batch to batch.

Tip

IF YOU GET CONCRETE ON YOUR HANDS, wash it off promptly. Follow up with vinegar at the end of the day. An acid, vinegar counteracts the alkalinity of cement and keeps your skin from chafing.

Calculating quantities

Before you decide whether to mix concrete yourself or have it delivered, you must determine how much you'll need. Use math or muscle to figure out the volume.

For the math method, multiply your object's length times width times height. Measure in feet and fractions of a foot, as labels on bagged mixes state their yield in cubic feet. Divide the total by 27 to convert to cubic yards, the number that a delivery company would want. To estimate quantities with complex molds, mentally divide the object into simple shapes and calculate their volumes individually. Or use the muscle method: Measure how much sand fits inside the mold.

A 5-gallon bucket is a useful measure. It holds two-thirds of a cubic foot— the volume of a 5-square-foot counter that's 1½ inches thick.

TAKING PRECAUTIONS

Cement is dusty when dry and caustic when damp, and cement mixtures often contain considerable quantities of crystalline silica, which can damage your lungs. Wear a disposable respirator (the two-strap kind) when you work with dry ingredients. Whether you are handling dry mix or wet concrete, always wear rubber gloves, and add boots if needed. Eye protection is smart too. Check the top of your gloves and rubber boots frequently for unnoticed spills that may cause blisters you won't feel at first. Rinse off any spills promptly. Cement burns aren't trivial—they can require treatment at a burn center.

RIGHT: *If you use liquid pigment, rinse the jar directly over the container where you are measuring water for your mix. This lets you use all of the pigment you bought, helps ensure consistent color from batch to batch, and eliminates the risk that you'll pollute nearby streams by spilling wash water on the ground.*

Pigments

When you work with dry pigments, wear a disposable mask. Never wash pigments into storm drains or waterways, and be especially careful with green and blue. They probably contain chromium, copper, or cobalt—all heavy metals that are extremely toxic to aquatic life. Collect all wash water and solids and use them in a later batch of concrete, if possible. Otherwise, leave the water in plastic tubs and let it evaporate. Dispose of the solids at an approved landfill.

Acid stains

Acid stains contain hydrochloric acid and other hazardous ingredients. Read labels and follow all instructions. Protect your skin, eyes, and lungs when you apply the product. Wear goggles and neoprene gloves. Depending on the situation, you may also need a protective apron and boots as well as a full-face mask fitted with acid/gas cartridges. As with other acids, add the stain to water, not water to the stain, or the solution may spatter or boil. Proper disposal of containers and rinse water is very important.

LEFT: *Cement is about as caustic as lye, so it's crucial to pay attention to safety. You need a mask only when you are working with dry material, but you should wear gloves whether the mix is wet or dry.*

CHOOSING A SCRATCH RECIPE

There are literally hundreds of different formulas for concrete. But for projects like those in this book, two basic recipes work well. As you gain experience, you can adjust them to create specialty mixes.

The two basic recipes differ primarily in the size of aggregate they contain. Basic Concrete Mix contains gravel, so it's suitable for projects such as countertops or pathways that are at least 2 inches thick. For thinner slabs and projects that call for sculpting or carving, use Basic Sand Mix.

The recipes call for "parts" of various ingredients. Think of a part as a measuring cup that can change size according to the scale of the project. For small tiles, you might make one part equal to one cup. For a countertop, it might mean one 5-gallon bucket.

BASIC CONCRETE MIX

- ❖ ½ part cement
- ❖ 1 part pea gravel (⅜ inch or less)
- ❖ 1 part sand
- ❖ Approximately ¼ part water

Yield: about 1½ parts concrete

BASIC SAND MIX

- ❖ 1 part cement
- ❖ 2 parts sand
- ❖ Approximately ½ part water

Yield: about 2 parts sand mix

Cement options

If you want to use what's available at standard building-materials stores, look for the standard gray cement, which may be labeled Type I (general purpose) or Type I-II (similar but more resistant to breaking down). Be sure to ask for cement, not concrete, which already has aggregate mixed in. If you want white cement, which can be tinted to brighter colors, you might need to hunt it down at masonry suppliers or ready-mix-concrete companies.

If you develop your skills and become interested in casting intricate shapes, you may also want to incorporate small amounts of specialty cements, such as fly ash or metakaolin (see Resources, pages

For thick objects like this fountain, use Basic Concrete Mix. Gravel in the mix strengthens the concrete and interlocks in a way that helps hold the object together.

188–189). Known as pozzolans, these fine powders act like miniature BBs, helping other ingredients slip into place with less water. (Or purchase special countertop mixes, which already include them.) If you are spending the extra money for white cement, you may wish to avoid using fly ash, which is dark or tan. The material does have good environmental benefits, though, because it's a recycled product collected from smokestacks at coal-burning power plants. Metakaolin, which is made from purified kaolin clay, is white and doesn't change the way pigments tint white cement. Mixing metakaolin with gray cement lightens colors slightly.

Aggregate options

Look for mason's sand or all-purpose sand. Avoid play sand, which has round grains of fairly uniform size. With sand, as with gravel, a mixture of sizes works better because the smaller particles settle in around the larger ones. Order aggregate by the size of the largest particles you want. For example, "one-fourth minus" means a range of sand and gravel sizes from 1/4-inch diameter down to grains almost too fine to see. If you want gravel about all the same size, perhaps to scatter on the surface, the term to use is "neat," as in "one-fourth neat" to get gravel all about 1/4 inch in diameter.

Unless you are scattering gravel on the surface, select a type with sharp edges, if you have a choice. The sharp-edged kinds have been blasted at a quarry or crushed. They pack tighter than rounded gravel, which is shaped by glaciers or flowing water.

The biggest particles should not exceed one-fifth the thickness of the object you are forming. For thin pieces, you might need particles no more than 1/8 inch or less. But paths, floors, and thick areas such as hearths benefit from larger gravel. Go up to 3/4 inch for a 4-inch slab.

For projects that will have a polished terrazzo-like finish, Basic Sand Mix is a good choice. You'd need to do a lot more grinding to create a good-looking surface on concrete made with gravel.

With white cement, you might also want to use white aggregate, such as crushed limestone (dolomite or calcite) or quartzite sands.

Water and its substitutes

Incorporating just the right amount of water is crucial. If there is too little, the mix will be hard to form and trowel smooth. When the mold comes off, there may be air gaps along edges. But if there is too much water, it will work its way to the surface as you trowel, especially if you begin too soon. Tiny tunnels left by the water will remain when the mix hardens. They make concrete porous and susceptible to staining and frost damage.

When you mix concrete, resist the temptation to add more water than the recipe calls for. Adding more water does make concrete easier to shape, but it's a shortcut that can come back to haunt you. Add just enough water when you are combining ingredients to make the concrete workable.

To make concrete flow well with less water, substitute acrylic or latex fortifier (also sold as bonding adhesive) for all or part of the water. Replacing half the water with fortifier gives great results, but you can use less to save money or more to make the concrete denser or to help it bond to existing concrete.

VARYING THE BASIC RECIPES

You can tweak the recipes on page 52 in several ways:

❖ Add ½ part more cement plus a little additional water to create a creamier cement. *Benefit:* produces a smoother finish with less effort.

❖ Replace up to half the water with acrylic or latex fortifier. *Benefit:* creates denser concrete that's less porous and less likely to crack. For sand mix, also allows applications ½ to 1 inch thick.

❖ Add polypropylene fibers. *Benefit:* protects against surface cracks. For sand mix, also adds stiffness.

❖ Replace part of the cement (up to 15 percent) with fly ash or metakaolin and reduce the amount of water. *Benefit:* makes concrete denser, easier to shape, and less prone to surface cracks.

ABOVE: *Except for small steppingstones, exterior paving needs to be at least 4 inches thick or it's likely to crack. That makes Basic Concrete Mix the right choice.*

BELOW: *Basic Sand Mix allows you to create thin objects—or thin layers, as in this table, which was designed so that it would look rough yet have a smooth writing surface on top. A gravel mix does not work on thin pours, because there isn't enough vertical space for the larger particles to be surrounded by enough concrete. They would create weak spots where the concrete might crack. The diameter of the largest aggregate should be no more than one-fifth the thickness of the layer.*

Creating freeze-resistant concrete

Ice crystals occupy about 9 percent more space than the water that's in them. So when concrete absorbs water and then freezes, the ice can split the concrete. There are some ways to eliminate or at least reduce this danger:

❖ *Replace some of the mix water with acrylic or latex fortifier.*

❖ *Barely dampen the concrete and pound it into place (see pages 73 and 166–167).*

❖ *Add an "air-entraining" product. Available from concrete-supply companies, this material forms tiny bubbles that act as safety valves, giving ice crystals room to expand. Requires truck delivery or motorized mixing.*

❖ *Use a bagged mix that contains waterproofing ingredients.*

❖ *Coat the cured concrete with a sealer.*

SELECTING BAGGED MIXES

Bagged mixes free you from searching for specialty ingredients and from buying them in greater quantities than you need. Manufacturers rarely reveal what's in their mixes, so go by other characteristics, such as suitable thickness or speed of setting, to select the best type for your project.

❖ If you're trying to decide between two products, look on the label or instruction sheet for the strength (shown as psi, or pounds per square inch). Although this number refers only to crush resistance, you can use it as an overall indicator of durability and abrasion resistance.

❖ The depth limits on the label indicate the maximum size of aggregate in the mix. Concrete sold for slabs more than 2 inches thick contains gravel up to $\frac{1}{2}$ inch across. Sand mixes designed for $\frac{1}{16}$-inch applications use finer grit than those for $\frac{1}{2}$-inch layers.

Always check labels to determine whether to use procedures different from those shown with the projects in this book, which were created with the recipes or bagged mixes noted in the text. Other bagged mixes might work, but it may be difficult to determine whether similar-sounding products from different companies are identical. Call manufacturers' help lines (see Resources, pages 188–189) if you are not sure. One general caution: do not use acrylic or latex fortifier with bagged mixes that call for adding only water.

Using bagged mixes costs more than mixing concrete from scratch but makes it easier to achieve consistent results from batch to batch. That's especially important on projects like this fireplace hearth, surround, and mantel, which involve too many parts for one or even two people to cast all at once. These pieces were made with a bagged countertop mix and several shades of pigment.

Decoding bagged mixes

In some building-supply stores, an entire aisle is devoted to bagged concrete mixes. It can be difficult to decipher what's in the bags and which product will work best for a specific project. Here's a start.

CONCRETE MIX

❖ Gray portland cement, sand, and gravel

❖ Good for paths, steppingstones, and other projects at least 2 inches thick

❖ For countertops or other high-impact, smooth projects, add 1/2 gallon cement powder per sack of mix

CONCRETE COUNTER MIX

❖ White portland cement, sand, marble dust, metakaolin, and other ingredients

❖ Designed for countertops but has many other uses

❖ Can be mixed quite dry and pressed into shape

❖ White color tints well

❖ Polish for a terrazzo look

QUICK COUNTERTOP MIX

❖ Quick-setting portland cements, sands, and aggregates in Part A, plus additives, fibers and bonders with the correct amount of liquid in Part B

❖ No additional water is needed, so each batch is consistent

❖ Suitable only for casting upside down in a mold

❖ Sets in 30 minutes; remove from the mold in three hours and begin polishing in four hours

❖ Self-consolidating; no need to vibrate to remove air pockets

SAND MIX

❖ Gray portland cement and sand, in a ratio of approximately 1 to 3

❖ Good for countertops and other poured projects less than 2 inches thick

❖ Can also be used as a 1/2-inch or thicker coating for old concrete

❖ Can be carved, stamped, or sculpted

NON-SHRINK PRECISION GROUT

❖ Gray portland cement, sand, expansive materials, and other additives

❖ Develops high strength even when mixed quite soupy, so it flows into intricate molds

❖ Great for precast countertops

❖ Must be mixed mechanically

❖ Stiffens in 15 to 25 minutes, depending on temperature

FAST-SETTING CONCRETE MIX

❖ Gray portland cement, sand, and additives

❖ Sculpt as it begins to harden

❖ Or pour into a form, unmold when set, and carve details

❖ Stiffens in just 5 to 10 minutes; mix small batches

HIGH EARLY STRENGTH CONCRETE MIX

❖ Gray portland cement, sand, gravel, and additives

❖ Good for countertops, hearths, and other poured projects at leasl 2 inches thick

❖ Contains a higher than usual percentage of cement, so it's easier to finish

GLASS BLOCK MORTAR MIX

❖ Fine silica sand, mason's lime, white cement, and waterproofing ingredients

❖ Use as a topping on projects not subject to abrasion; too soft for casting

❖ White color works well with pigments

CONCRETE RESURFACER

❖ Gray portland cement, sand, polymers, and other ingredients

❖ Gives a fresh cement-based coat to old concrete

❖ Mix thin and spread by squeegee or brush, or add less water and trowcl on up to ½ inch deep

❖ Can be tinted and textured; suitable for layering different colors

Overview

These are the tools needed for paddle mixing. The drill part of a paddle mixer has side handles, which help the operator move the tool up and down. The red plastic barrel has a capacity of 19 gallons—big enough for two 70-pound bags of countertop mix. The oversized measuring cup helps ensure that the right amount of water is added to each batch.

CHOOSING A MIXING METHOD

The best method depends on how much concrete you are mixing, how often you plan to do it, and how much money you are willing to spend to ease your work. Most tool-rental companies carry portable and paddle-type mixers, and building-materials stores sell them.

Portable mixers

One with a 3.5-cubic-foot capacity will handle several bags of concrete. Standard models have a revolving drum, which mixes well when gravel is among the ingredients. Put in about three-fourths of the water first, along with liquid pigment if you are using it. Add gravel, then any dry pigment, followed by sand and finally cement, mixing after each addition. After you add the cement, squirt one burst of water into the mixer to reduce dust and prevent clumps. Tilt the tub back and forth periodically as the machine mixes. Add the final water in small amounts until the mixture has the consistency of oatmeal.

When sand is the only aggregate in a concrete mix, it tends to become plastered on the side of the drum. A better option is the type of portable mixer that masons use to prepare mortar. Mortar mixers have blades that turn inside the drum.

Paddle mixers

These consist of an eggbeater-type paddle powered by a heavy-duty drill. You pour most of the liquid into a bucket or tub with a capacity greater than the amount you are mixing. Add the dry ingredients, then direct the paddle up and down into the mix. Add the remaining water and mix again.

For hand mixing, work in a mortar tray or wheelbarrow. With a shovel or hoe, pull the dry mixture into the water little by little. Work the dampened material back toward the dry area, almost as you would when kneading bread. With the tool blade, repeatedly slice through the mixture to break up any lumps.

Hand mixing

For this method, you need only a hoe or shovel, plus a wheelbarrow or a mortar tray. Because a wheelbarrow is elevated, while a tray rests on the ground, each allows a different working angle. Experiment to discover which you prefer. Pour the dry ingredients into one end and the water into the other. Gradually work the dry material into the moist area. For extremely small batches, you can mix with gloved hands in an old plastic dishpan.

Choosing pigment

Buy pigment dispersed in water or as dry powder. Using the liquid form helps ensure even color. However, the widest color selection is available as powder, which is sold in bulk and in bags that disintegrate in a mixer. If you are using dry pigment and want to avoid streaks, stir it into some of the mix water with a whisk or an old, thick paintbrush, or use an old blender that you no longer use for food. If you are using a motorized mixer and a recipe with gravel, dump the pigment into the mixer after you add the stones. As they tumble, they will pulverize clumps of powder and disperse it. If you want streaks of color, stir dry pigment into the other ingredients after they are thoroughly mixed. Colors lighten as concrete cures, so at first expect to see a darker color than you want in the end.

ONE LAST CHECK

Before you mix concrete, step back and make sure everything is ready.

Forms or molds

❖ Sturdy enough?

❖ Level or (for outdoor projects) at proper angle for water to run off?

❖ Faucet and sink knockouts or other special features in place?

❖ Reinforcing cut to shape and rebar fully supported?

❖ Forms coated with oil or other form-release material?

❖ Surrounding areas protected with plastic?

❖ Tools at hand for vibrating air bubbles out of the mix?

Mixing and pouring

❖ Materials on hand: cement, aggregate, measured amount of mix water, additives (fortifiers, fibers, pigment, etc.), decorative material such as inlays?

❖ Tools and containers ready and in useable condition: cement mixer, paddle mixer, wheelbarrow or dishpan, shovel or hoe, hose and buckets, smoothing tools (flat board for initial leveling, wood and/or metal floats, edger)?

❖ Safety gear available: disposable respirator, rubber gloves, goggles?

Follow-up

❖ Plastic cover to keep project damp?

❖ Person assigned to rinse tools and containers promptly?

❖ Storage system planned for rinse water, especially if there are additives that should not go into soil?

Overview

Learning from a pro

FOLLOW ALONG AS BUDDY RHODES, a pioneer of decorative concrete, and his crew show the detailed steps needed to complete a 52-by-32-inch tabletop. As you see how a tabletop takes shape, you will learn tips Rhodes has gleaned during decades of making a wide array of concrete objects. Once you understand the basics, you'll be ready to try the projects described in the following chapters.

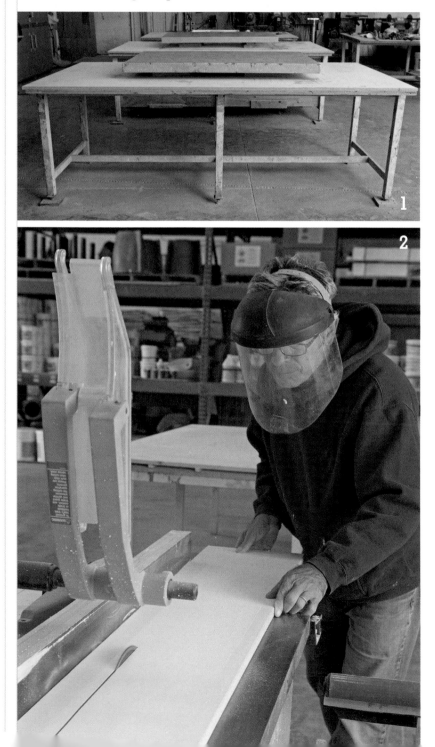

THE WORKTABLE

Rhodes works on tables 4 feet wide and 8 feet long, each supported by three pairs of steel legs welded to a top frame. He covers the base with one sheet of ¾-inch plywood plus one sheet of ¾-inch melamine-coated particleboard. The top sheet, which he replaces frequently, serves as the bottom of his molds. Rhodes shims the legs to make the tabletops perfectly level.

BUILDING THE MOLD

Rhodes chooses the right-side-up method to build the table, so the mold is very simple: just a big open box. He uses the sheet of melamine on his worktable as the bottom of the mold and screws the sides to that. The width of the sidepieces matches the thickness of the table—at least along the edges. To keep the weight down and to provide the form for a lip that will fit over the table's metal base, Rhodes slips a piece of plastic foam into the center of the mold and screws it into place. Because of the foam, the tabletop will wind up thinner in the center than along the edges, so it will look thicker than it is.

1 Rhodes' worktables have steel legs spaced about 4 feet apart and two sheets of ¾-inch-thick material on top. The tabletops in this picture were cast the previous day, directly on the top sheet of each table. Before this picture was taken, Rhodes elevated them on blocks so they would dry evenly on both sides.

2 On a table saw, Rhodes cuts melamine-coated particleboard into strips 2½ inches wide. This is the thickness of the table along the edges. Then he moves to a chop saw and cuts two pieces to the length of the table and two pieces to its width plus a few inches for overlap.

3 Rhodes uses a drill press to drill pilot holes in the sides (a hand-held drill also works). He makes one hole near each end and one every 16 inches or so in the middle. He widens the top of each hole with a counter-bore and drives the screw heads below the surface.

4 Screws must be long enough to bite into the particleboard base but not so long that they go through it. For 2½-inch-wide sides, Rhodes uses 3-inch screws.

5 Screwing sidepieces into place seems like a simple step, but Rhodes knows to prevent problems by snugging long pieces against a straight-edge so they don't bow. He also checks corners with a carpenter's square.

6 To make the table 1 inch thinner in the middle than it is along the sides, Rhodes uses inexpensive foam board to fill the bottom of the mold, except for a 1-inch border around the sides. He scores a line in the foam with a putty knife, then snaps the sides apart, as if cutting drywall.

7 Using a 1-inch spacer to ensure an even gap around the edges, Rhodes screws the foam to the bottom of the mold.

8 Dabs of clay protect screw heads so they're easy to remove later.

9 Rhodes chooses expanded-metal lath as reinforcing for this project to keep the tabletop intact while he's moving it around. It doesn't need rigid reinforcing because it will sit on sturdy metal legs. To determine where to cut the lath, Rhodes slips a sheet into the empty mold. With tin snips, he trims the mesh so it's 1 inch smaller than the mold on every side. Then he sets the mesh aside.

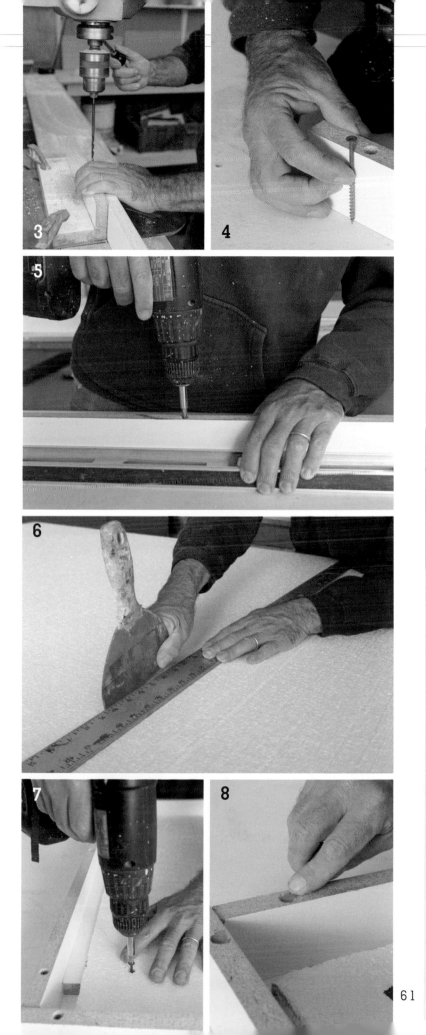

MIXING THE CONCRETE

Once you add water to cement, you are no longer the master of your time. If you want the project to turn out right, let the needs of the concrete dictate your work pace.

Rhodes wants to give the tabletop he's building a hand-troweled surface. That involves several steps, some of which can't occur until the concrete is rather stiff. So if he wants to be finished by 5 or 6 P.M. on a mild-temperature day, he starts mixing before noon. In cold weather, concrete stiffens more slowly. In hot weather, it sets faster.

Rhodes also knows that it's safer to have a helper, even for a job as small as a tabletop. One person mixes the concrete and cleans up tools and containers while the other person concentrates on placing and smoothing the concrete.

1 To combine liquid ingredients, Rhodes' assistant pours a jar of pigment into a large measuring container, then adds enough water to get 11 quarts. That's the lower end of what the concrete mix label recommends for two bags when a project will have a hand-troweled finish. (Some finishes require a stiffer mix.)

2 Trying to minimize dust, he dumps in one bag of dry mix.

3 In about a minute, the paddle mixer churns the mix into a lump-free slurry that resembles gravy.

4 The second bag of dry mix goes in, and the paddle mixer is switched back into action. It's a lot like mixing cookie dough, except that it takes muscle power to move the beater up and down. At first, the mix seems much too dry.

5 But after a few more minutes of mixing, the consistency proves to be just right. The mixture isn't soupy; it seems more like soft clay.

Evaluating stiffness

The trickiest aspect of mixing concrete is adding the right amount of water. One minute, the mixture seems too stiff. So you add a bit more water. Then, suddenly, it's too gooey. Test the consistency with a simple slump test. Cut the bottom off a foam or plastic cup and set the cup upside down. Fill it with concrete, tamping as you go. Lift the cup straight up. For sculpting or packing against a mold, the concrete should stay about the same height as the cup. If the pile slumps to about three-fourths of the cup's height, the mix is right for pouring into a form. If it slumps more, add more dry mix. If it slumps less, add water.

PLACING AND LEVELING CONCRETE

Chemical bonds begin forming as soon as water contacts cement. Ensure a strong result by minimizing your handling of the damp concrete. Work quickly and shovel or dump the material as close as possible to where it's needed in the mold.

For most projects, fill the mold partway, taking care to pack concrete into edges and around detail areas, such as faucet knockouts. Add metal reinforcement if your project requires it, and then finish filling the mold. The mold should wind up slightly overfull.

1 Once the concrete is mixed, it needs to be moved close to the mold. A simple cart with casters eliminates heavy lifting.

2 Rhodes begins to spread concrete across the bottom of the mold. He sets down big handfuls and smooths out the material with his gloved hands.

3 Along edges, Rhodes builds up a thick layer of concrete. Because voids would be especially noticeable here, he takes special care to tamp the concrete thoroughly. He levels other areas by using his hand like a trowel.

4 Into the half-filled mold, Rhodes lowers the sheet of expanded-metal lath that he cut earlier. He works it into the surface and covers it with a thin layer of concrete. Over that, he adds the rest of the concrete.

5 With a straight 2 by 4, Rhodes begins to level the concrete. Resting the screed on the sides of the mold, he saws back and forth, leaving a shallow zigzag trail from a knot on the edge of the board. Where there is too little concrete, Rhodes tosses on a little more and uses the screed again.

6 After Rhodes has made several passes with the screed, the countertop becomes level. The zigzags and other rough lines at this point are not a problem. In fact, it would be worse to try to smooth them out, as troweling this early would bring water to the surface and weaken the concrete.

7 As soon as the concrete is level, Rhodes picks up an orbital sander, slips it into a plastic bag to keep the wet concrete off it, and begins to coax bubbles out of the mix by letting the sander oscillate against the sides of the mold. When bubbles appear, Rhodes moves on to the next area.

SMOOTHING AND FINISHING

The key to achieving a smooth, durable finish on concrete is not rushing to begin troweling. Wait for the surface water to disappear and for the concrete to lose its sheen. Depending on the mix and the weather, you may need to wait 30 minutes to several hours.

Float first

Creating a hand-troweled surface requires several steps, with time between each one. Use a wooden or magnesium float for the first pass, which should occur only after water on the surface has disappeared. The goal of this step is to make the surface even more level. Push any protruding aggregate below the top skim of cement paste, then patch any divots you see. For patch material, use leftover concrete mix or some of the paste that dribbled over the outside of the mold. The concrete should become smooth but still look slightly textured when you finish floating. Stop at this point if you want a nonskid surface or if you plan to finish the concrete with a broom or other texture tool.

Trowel, then trowel again

Wait another hour or so for the concrete to become even stiffer. Then switch to a metal trowel and work the surface again. Hold the leading edge up and press down harder than you did the first time. Stop at this step for a pleasantly smooth surface on an object such as a garden bench.

For a glossy surface, trowel again two or three more times but wait a while between passes. Gradually increase the angle of the trowel so that you are holding the leading edge even higher and pressing down even more each time.

ENSURING SLOW, EVEN DRYING

The chemical bonds that make concrete hard continue to form for weeks after a piece is poured, provided it remains moist. To keep concrete from drying too fast, people often spread plastic sheeting over it. However, especially with tinted concrete, condensation that forms on the plastic may drip onto the concrete and cause streaks. White mineral deposits, known as efflorescence, can also form. For projects built right side up, avoid these problems by keeping the concrete damp with mist rather than plastic. Plastic is fine, though, for projects cast upside down in a mold.

Troweled-in color

If you want variegated color, consider troweling pigment into the surface as the concrete stiffens. Use premixed color hardener or make your own from pigment, cement, and sand in a 1:6:6 ratio. Reduce the amount of pigment if you wish. A home-made mix won't produce color that looks as uniform or trowels on as smoothly, because the pigment and cement can't be combined as thoroughly as they are in the manufactured versions.

To broadcast dry pigment, place the concrete and roughly level it as you would any slab. Sprinkle on about two-thirds of the pigment mixture. Trowel it in, wait for surface water to disappear, then add the rest of the colorant and trowel the surface again.

Umber color hardener transforms newly poured gray concrete. The commercially prepared mixture of powdered pigment, cement and other ingredients was sprinkled on dry soon after the concrete was poured. Troweling works it into the surface and incorporates enough water from the underlying concrete so that the cement in the topping will harden. The resulting concrete will be not only more colorful but also more abrasion-resistant.

1 An hour or so after screeding, Rhodes goes over the surface again, this time with a long wooden float. He works in a circular pattern and tries to feel where the low and high spots are so he can even them out.

2 Where divots appear, Rhodes adds a little leftover concrete mix. He smooths over the patches with his float.

3 Rhodes waits another hour, then picks up his steel trowel. He works the surface again, always moving in circular paths so that any trowel marks on the finished counter won't be straight lines, which look jarring.

4 By the final troweling, the surface is smooth and almost glossy.

5 When Rhodes has troweled for the final time, he lets the surface dry slowly overnight. To keep the concrete from drying too quickly, he mists it with water periodically. Because this table has a troweled surface, Rhodes doesn't cover it with plastic. He has seen instances in which condensation on the back of plastic dripped onto the concrete and left permanent marks.

Concrete surfaces undergo a remarkable transition between the end of the floating step (top) and the end of the first troweling (bottom).

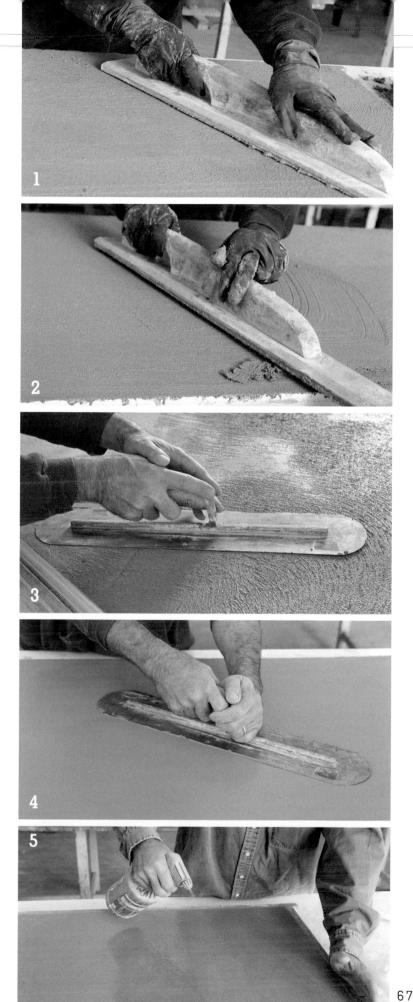

67

REMOVING THE MOLD

Concrete usually needs just a few hours to become stiff enough for the mold to come off, but it's too fragile at that point to be lifted or moved around. Rhodes waits until the day after he pours. He could wait longer, though he's found that flat objects like this tabletop sometimes warp if one side dries faster than the other. To prevent that, he takes off the mold and elevates the concrete, allowing both sides to dry evenly.

The concrete is completely stiff at this point, but it's still relatively weak. It won't reach full strength for about four weeks. So Rhodes gets a helper when he moves the piece.

1 First Rhodes removes the screws holding the mold sides in place.

2 He then slips a wide putty knife under one edge. If the edge is sealed shut, he taps on the workbench with a rubber mallet to break the seal, then slips the blade in.

3 Rhodes and his helper slide the tabletop toward them just far enough so one edge overhangs the edge of the workbench. Then, in one smooth movement, they tip the slab upright. The screws holding the foam insert in place automatically pop loose, and the foam stays along for the ride.

4 Rhodes sets out four pairs of short 2 by 4s, and he and his assistant lower the tabletop onto them. The blocks allow air to circulate evenly around the edge of the table so it does not warp.

REMOVING ROUGH SPOTS

On day three, the final steps take place. Rhodes uses a light touch to preserve the look and feel of the hand-troweled finish.

5 Wearing a disposable respirator, Rhodes lightly polishes the top with 220-grit aluminum oxide sandpaper, the same kind used on wood. He makes a few passes over each section, just enough to make the surface feel smooth.

6 With an abrasive brick, Rhodes chamfers the corners, keeping the brick tipped about 45 degrees. He doesn't try to round over the corners at this point for fear of gouging the top surface with the brick, which cuts aggressively. He chamfers the bottom edge of the tabletop as well.

7 With a green diamond pad, he removes the rough surface left by the abrasive brick. He also rounds over the chamfer, creating an edge that feels nicely finished.

8 One little detail remains: removing the foam on the back. Rhodes tips the tabletop over again, but this time he sets it down on foam blocks to protect the top surface. As if shoveling snow, he scoops out the foam with a wide putty knife. Pieces come out in messy chunks.

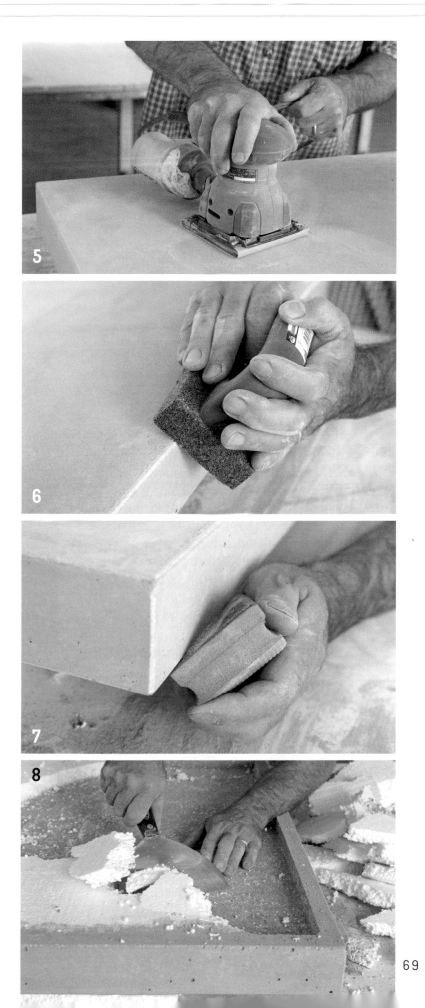

Overview

69

If you want to carve or sculpt large pieces, reduce the amount of concrete you need by filling some of the space at the center with foam. Buy blocks of polystyrene foam at packing-supply companies or build up thick pieces from foam insulation board layered with double-stick tape. Cut the foam with a bread knife, drywall saw, or other long-blade tool. If you need to refine the shape, use a wire brush or a rasp. Wrap the form with metal mesh and weave in 20-gauge wire to hold the mesh in place. Cover the mesh with a sand-and-cement mixture, as if you were plastering a wall. The first layer will look messy, but you can continue adding layers. Sculpt and carve them as you build up the shape.

CARVING CONCRETE

You can also shape concrete by carving it. The effect looks very much like carved stone, but the effort it takes is far less. If you carve your design when the concrete is stiff but not yet very hard, you won't generate dust and you won't need special stone-carving tools. A kitchen knife, a spoon, an old saw blade, or a nail will work fine. As the piece becomes harder and harder, you can add progressively finer details and create an even smoother surface.

Pour a carving blank

Start by making the concrete block or slab that you will carve. Use Basic Sand Mix (page 52), a bagged sand mix, or quick-setting cement if you want your object to have a somewhat rough texture. The uniformity of the sand and the typical size of the grains influence the amount of fine detail that you will be able to create. For fine details or a smooth surface, first sieve the dry ingredients through window screen to remove large particles. For an ultrasmooth, glistening surface, prepare Basic Sand Mix but substitute finely ground marble dust for the sand and use latex or acrylic bonding compound.

Timing

If you plan to use carving techniques to add details, remember that concrete is easiest to carve soon after it sets. But since it won't have developed much strength at that point, treat the piece gently. If you are using a mold, design it so you can pull away the sides and begin carving without moving the piece from its base. On a 70-degree day, it may take three hours for a standard sand mix to stiffen enough to carve. Quick-setting cement may be ready in half an hour. In most cases, you'll have at least several hours to carve. After that, you will still be able to polish rough edges, but it will be difficult to alter the basic shape.

Techniques

To give your piece a uniform texture, scrape off the crusty surface cement with a serrated knife or a reciprocating saw. Or leave some areas untouched to create contrasting textures. Carve the main shape with a knife. Refine details with other tools as needed. When you're done, lightly brush the surface with a whisk broom or a toothbrush, depending on the piece's size. Cover the object with plastic and keep it damp.

As the concrete hardens, you can add finer details and smooth the surface with a rasp, sanding sponge, or wet-dry sandpaper. To keep dust down, work on a damp surface.

ABOVE, TOP: *Concrete that's stiff but not yet hard is ready to carve. A kitchen knife slices through a design outlined with a clipped-off nail in a wooden handle.*

ABOVE, BOTTOM: *To color the carving, the artist mixed equal amounts of white cement and pigment and sprinkled them onto the still-damp concrete. After dribbling water onto the pigment, the surface was smoothed with a butter knife.*

You can use common tools to carve concrete while it's still relatively soft.

Patterns and styles

Mention "decorative concrete" to some people and they'll assume you're talking about large expanses of paving stamped and colored to look like stone or brick. That is indeed one of the possibilities. But concrete also adapts to a wide variety of other surface treatments, including many that do not require expensive, specialized equipment. In this chapter, you will see examples of finishes that you can use on a wide variety of projects. The smooth finishes are suitable for countertops, tabletops, and sinks. Save the heavily textured or surface-pigmented finishes for wall tiles, fireplace surrounds, garden art such as fountain backsplashes, and similar uses where the surface won't wear down or become clogged with dirt. One caveat: to keep people from slipping, avoid overly smooth surfaces on floors or paving that may become wet.

Terrazzo

To create classic terrazzo, embed marble chips or mother-of-pearl in a cement mix and grind the surface smooth. Large projects are best done by pros with multihead polishing machines. But you can tackle small projects yourself if you're willing to accept slight indentations and have access to a hand-held grinder or stone polisher equipped for wet sanding with diamond pads. If you do it yourself, lay out the design so you can divide large areas with metal gauge strips, which also set the depth and control cracks. Combine marble dust, marble chips, and cement in equal proportions. Mix with water and concrete bonding adhesive into a stiff goo. Smooth over dampened concrete. Keep damp 3 days, then polish wet. Start with 50-grit pads and go to 400 or higher.

THIS SAMPLE:
White cement, white marble dust, black and green marble chips, mother-of-pearl; Davis Colors #3685 green added to two sections in different concentrations; brass strips

Glass terrazzo

THIS SAMPLE:
Buddy Rhodes Concrete Countertop Mix plus Davis Colors #6058 reddish-brown; confetti glass shards

Press glass shards into freshly poured concrete to create another type of terrazzo. Place a paper pattern on the surface to confine the glass to the design area. Embed the pieces with a trowel and force some of the surface cream over them. Trowel smooth. Wait 3 days, then polish. This sample was created with stained-glass waste and Buddy Rhodes Concrete Countertop Mix, which incorporates marble chips. A 50-grit hand diamond pad exposed the marble in this mix, creating a subdued terrazzo effect overall. Exposing the pattern took more work. We used a stone polisher.

YOU NEED:

- ❖ Basic Sand Mix, page 52, or bagged sand mix
- ❖ Dry or liquid pigment
- ❖ Concrete bonding adhesive (over old concrete or if final step is delayed)
- ❖ Paper pattern
- ❖ Cooking-oil spray
- ❖ Carving tools or margin trowel
- ❖ Trowel

Fill a carved design with a contrasting color of sand m to create a pattern that wo wear off. For the base colo spread sand mix at least ½ inch thick over existing concrete or pour a slab tha at least 1½ inches thick. C a paper template with hol where the contrasting colo will be. Oil the pattern ar

YOU NEED:

- ❖ Bagged concrete resurfacing material
- ❖ Dry or liquid pigment, if desi
- ❖ Squeegee of a size suitable for your project
- ❖ Paddle mixer, drill, and 5-ga bucket for mixing
- ❖ Cut-off nail pounded into a wooden handle
- ❖ Styrofoam pad
- ❖ Soft cloth

Scratch a design into a cement topping to give concrete the look of st Incorporate existing cr into your design becau will inevitably transfer

YOU NEED:

- ❖ Basic Sand Mix or Basic Concrete Mix, page 52, or a bagged mix (with ½ gallon added cement per bag if you use standard bagged concrete mix)
- ❖ Broken tiles
- ❖ Sponge, preferably hydrophobic polyester, the type sold at mason's-supply stores or for smoothing wallpaper; it rinses out easily

Set bits of tile or pottery into damp concrete or sand mix to create mosaic designs. You can also create mosaics with mastic and grout, as you would set tile, but the direct method allows you to embed a design in a small section of a path or other concrete project. Spread and level the concrete or sand mix. Dampen and place the

YOU NEED:

- ❖ Basic Sand Mix or Basic Concrete Mix, page 52, or a bagged mix (with about ½ gallon extra cement if you use standard concrete mix)
- ❖ Glass or other flat mosaic pieces
- ❖ Adhesive shelf paper

Place glass or other decorative bits into a mold to cast a mosaic design into a countertop or similar project that you make upside down. Use only absolutely flat pieces for this technique, and press them to adhesive shelf paper or attach with washable glue. Either step will keep the pieces from shifting and pre-

pieces, then jiggle each one to embed it fully. Smooth around edges with a barely damp sponge. Blot surrounding areas if you want to create a slightly textured surface. As the concrete stiffens, wipe tiles clean. Rinse and squeeze out the sponge frequently. Wipe surfaces gently; sand grains can scratch glazed tile.

vent cement from seeping underneath. As with any molded project, the design will appear in reverse, so adhere the surface you want to expose. When the design is in place, prepare a sand mix. Make hamburger-size patties and add them one by one. Pat each one down and jiggle the mold to make sure the mixture fills in around the edges of the mosaic.

Tile mosaic

THIS SAMPLE:
Basic Sand Mix made with half white and half gray cement; glazed tiles

Molded mosaic

THIS SAMPLE:
Basic Concrete Mix made with ¼-inch gravel and Davis Colors #860 black pigment; dichroic and cobalt-blue glass from Mesolini Glass Studio

Recipes

Inlays

THIS SAMPLE:
Bagged concrete mix prepared with additional ½ gallon white cement per bag and Davis Colors #3685 green; ¾-inch copper pipe

Carved de

*Basi
prepare
crete bondi
and Davis Colors #
bro*

Projects for your home and garden

Indoors and out, concrete can find a home at your house. Because of its incredible versatility, you may choose it for a simple project, such as a steppingstone, or for a far more elaborate project, such as a sink or fireplace surround. This chapter includes design ideas as well as step-by-step instructions for a range of projects. If you're new to working with concrete, you may want to start with projects such as the steppingstone path or any of the garden pots. Then move up to more challenging projects. Those shown here incorporate a variety of techniques, allowing you to adapt the directions to build other projects of your own design. You can also vary the surface treatments to incorporate features shown in the previous chapter.

Countertops

ABOVE: *The blue countertop and tub surround help set a playful tone in this children's bathroom.*

AMONG ALL THE WAYS to use decorative concrete indoors, countertops are probably the most popular. Concrete has the solid look of natural stone. But you pour it yourself or order it custom-made, so you can incorporate special features, such as an integral drainboard next to a sink. For the most scratch resistance, add metal trivets near a stove and use a finish in which most of the surface cement is sanded off, exposing aggregate underneath.

ABOVE, LEFT: *Several shades of gold combine on this island countertop, giving it an especially rich look. Besides providing a generous work area, the countertop doubles as a breakfast spot.*

ABOVE, RIGHT: *A copper edge band frames this island countertop. To create the marble effect, the builder mixed light-blue concrete and placed it in the form one handful at a time. After removing the mold, he filled voids with darker cement.*

RIGHT: *Curves are easy to create in concrete, and the shape makes a countertop such as this one especially useful as a place for guests to gather as dinner is being prepared. As with round dining tables, a curved counter always has room for one more person.*

OPPOSITE: *It's easy to add special features to concrete countertops. The owners of this kitchen collected and positioned maple leaves, then had them cast into place by the professional who built the countertop.*

TOP LEFT: *Six kinds of seashells and a starfish are found among the pebbles that adorn this bathroom countertop, which was built for a house near the Pacific Ocean. The contractor added black pigment to the concrete, scattered the shells, and coated the surface with an epoxy sealer.*

MIDDLE LEFT: *Black concrete and white concrete were mixed separately, then poured together to create the dramatic look of this outdoor countertop. The white portions were later stained to take on a reddish color.*

BOTTOM LEFT: *Too big to be cast in one piece, this island countertop consists of five sections with a diamond-shaped piece at the center. The installers filled the seams with grout so that the countertop would echo the look of the tile floor.*

TOP RIGHT: *Built for a vacation cottage by the beach, this thick concrete sink and countertop give an Asian flair to a small, spare bathroom.*

ABOVE: *Although it looks massive, the base of this kitchen island is made from relatively thin pieces of concrete that box in a support post that runs up the middle. A metal bracket, just visible underneath the overhang, supports the cantilever. Concrete countertops 1½ inches thick, like these, can extend out only about 10 inches without added support or cracks may develop. The countertop and base are both tinted a custom ash color and hand troweled.*

LEFT: *The custom edge on the countertop helps this kitchen island appear more like furniture than standard cabinetry.*

This project features a cast-in-place countertop with an optional terrazzo finish flecked with bits of white marble, mother-of-pearl, and cobalt-blue glass. Casting the countertop in place lets you skip both the heavy lifting and the "upside down and backward" thinking involved in precasting into a mirror-image mold. But troweling the surface smooth does require skill. Practice on other projects first.

A cast-in-place countertop

The countertop rests on a base of 1/2-inch-thick cement board, enabling you to keep the concrete 1 inch thick except at the edges, which are just deep enough to hide the cement board. The result is a normal-height countertop that's easily supported by standard cabinets. Reinforcing consists of galvanized-steel stucco lath, so you must use aggregate small enough to fit through the openings. We used Buddy Rhodes Concrete Counter Mix, which contains white cement and bits of white marble, but a standard sand mix would be fine. We troweled blue recycled glass and a few handfuls of mother-of-pearl into the surface and sanded it a few days later by hand, because a polishing machine would have made a mess in the room.

DIRECTIONS

1 Make a template by outlining the shape of your countertop on cardboard. The edges should be flush with the sides of the cabinet. If the counter is bigger than a sheet of cement board, mark joints on the template; they must be placed over cabinet walls. Also mark the sink outline using the template packaged with it.

2 Using the sink template as a guide, cut a plug from foam insulation at least 1½ inches thick to keep the sink free of concrete. A jigsaw or bandsaw works well. Sand edges of the foam and wrap them with plastic tape (see Step 5, page 108).

3 Cut the cement board to fit. For straight cuts, score a line with a utility knife or a knife made from cement board. Snap the sides into a fold and cut through the remaining mesh, as shown.

4 Cut curves with a jigsaw fitted with a wood blade. The blade will wear out fast; have a spare.

5 Along the top of the cabinet sides, screw on some scraps of wood flush with the cabinet top. Drape plastic over the cabinets and place the cement board on top. Then screw down through the board into the wood scraps using drywall screws. Attaching the board this way makes the counter easy to remove if you or a later owner wants to redecorate. Attach the foam plug in a similar way.

6 To guard against cracks appearing in the countertop, cover seams with the mesh tape sold for use with cement board. The tape has an adhesive backing, so it stays in place.

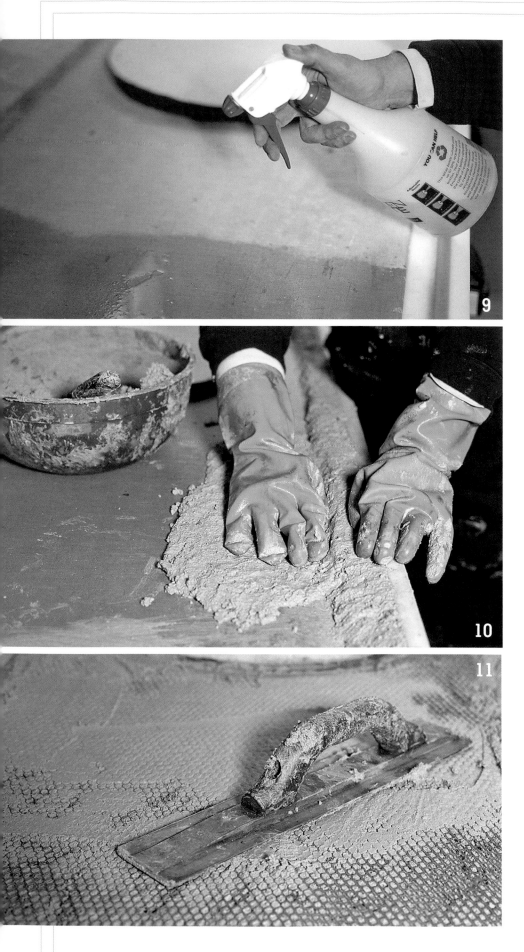

7 With aviator's snips, cut 2½-pound galvanized-steel stucco lath to match the countertop, minus a 1-inch gap along all edges, including all around the sink. If you need multiple pieces, overlap the lath by a few inches.

8 Tack a board 1 inch thick along the back edge to create a guide when you screed the concrete. Plan to cover this later with a back-splash.

9 Before you mix the concrete, dampen the cement board with water. If the cement board dries out, repeat this step just before you fill the form. But blot up any puddles.

10 Prepare Basic Sand Mix, page 52, or a bagged sand mix. With a putty knife, take a little of the prepared mix and press it down into seams covered with mesh. By hand, pack more of the mixture into the edge form. Work quickly to fill the rest of the form halfway.

11 Place the wire mesh. With a float, lightly press it into the bottom layer, just enough so the wire doesn't curl. Make sure it isn't too close to the edges. Then fill the form the rest of the way.

12 With a hammer or stick, tap along the edge band to release air bubbles. Then level the concrete with a straight board as you would for any poured project.

13 Sprinkle glass pieces, mother-of-pearl, or other inlays on the surface. (If you are not going for a terrazzo finish, see page 66 for tips on troweling a surface smooth.)

14 Embed the inlays by troweling over them. To eliminate gaps around their edges, trowel until they are completely covered with the cream of cement and fine sand that is on the surface.

15 Cover the countertop with plastic. For the next three days, periodically mist the concrete to keep it damp.

16 Remove the edge form and cut out the sink plug. Then begin polishing with wet-dry sandpaper, diamond pads, or solid aluminum-carbide blocks. Start with 100- or 120-grit abrasive and work up to 220 and then 440. If sanding ejects whole pieces of sand or other aggregate, delay this step for another day. Keep handy a pan of water and a sponge (preferably the type sold for masonry jobs) so you can keep the surface damp and periodically wipe away the slurry you will create. Stop sanding when you like the effect.

17 If you see gaps that you don't like, fill them with a paste of cement and water. Allow them to harden for a few days. Polish with wet-dry sandpaper.

18 Seal and wax the counter before you use it.

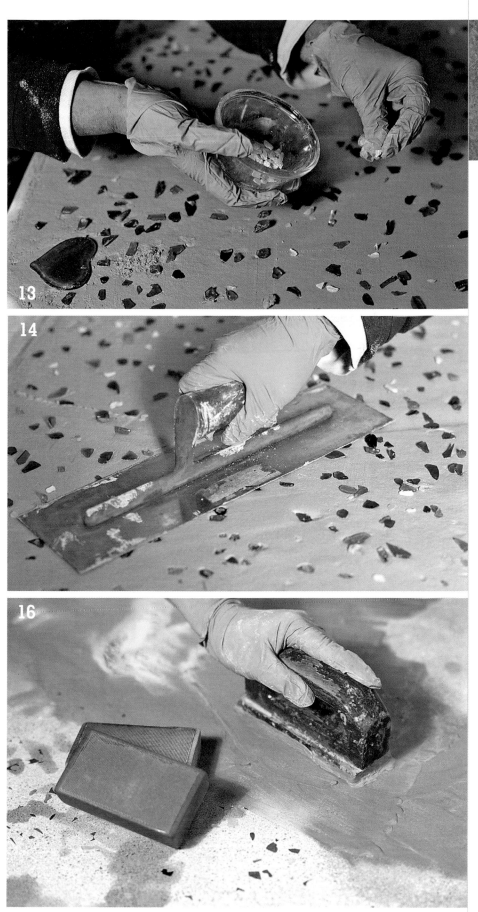

105

6 Trace the sink template onto 1½-inch-thick foam insulation and cut it out with a jigsaw or a box knife with the blade fully extended. Sand edges and cover with plastic tape. Also cut foam to fit snugly in the bowls. Smooth painter's tape around the top edges of the bowls. If there is a bevel, fill it with plasticine clay. Seal the edge between the sink and the cement board with a bead of caulk.

7 Screw the cement board to the cleats. Next to the sink, where you couldn't fit a screwdriver to loosen the cleats, use machine screws with wing nuts underneath. Cover joints, except at control joints, with mesh tape.

8 Build the edge form. For a bullnose edge, rip a length of 1½-inch drain-pipe on a table saw, using a featherboard to hold the pipe firmly to the fence. Build a wooden cradle for the pipe using a 1 by 3 for the vertical piece and a 2 by 2 for the base. Cut out part of the 2 by 2 so the pipe sits into it without leaving a lip. Clamp the cradle to the cabinets so the interior of the bullnose is flush with the bottom of the cement board.

9 Cut expanded-metal lath to fit with-in the form, staying 1 inch back from all edges. Reinforce skinny sections along the sink with thin mesh strips.

10 With the bowl forms snugged into place, carefully align the larger foam piece and screw the layers together. To keep the foam from lifting when you add the concrete mix, wedge pieces of wood between the foam and the ceiling using small pieces of wood at either end so you don't mar the ceiling or dig into the foam.

11 Plan how you will screed, or level, the concrete. You can run a board back and forth between the front edging and a guide board next to the wall at the back, but the front edge will wind up with a stepped-down edge because of the thickness of the pipe. For a smooth edge, screw the back guide board to the wall and notch the screed so its ends ride along the guide and the pipe and its middle section hangs down and smooths the surface. Make the drop-down section shorter than the counter's width so you can move the screed back and forth to level the concrete.

 12 With a spray bottle, thoroughly dampen the cement board.

13 Prepare Basic Sand Mix, page 52, or a bagged sand mix. Smooth some over the mesh tape, then spread about a ½-inch layer over the counter and pack the front edge thoroughly. Tamp the front edge with a hammer to release air bubbles.

14 Carefully lower the metal lath into place and finish filling the form. Screed it level.

15 Wait a little while and then smooth the surface with a wooden float. Wait a little longer and go over it again with a trowel. See page 66 for tips on achieving a smooth finish.

16 When the concrete stiffens, cover it with plastic and keep it damp for three days before removing the edge form and the foam pieces. Remove any rough spots with either a sanding sponge or a diamond pad.

17 Fill any holes along the sink or front edges with a paste of water and cement tinted to match. To smooth the bullnose patches, rub along the edge with a piece of plastic wrap or a sandwich bag.

18 Scrub away any concrete traces that seeped onto the sink. Polish the top with fine sandpaper or diamond polishing pads, starting with 120-grit if you want a terrazzo look and 220 if you want more of a troweled finish. Seal and wax the counter before you use it.

With a thin concrete overlay, you can transform an old tile countertop into one that's seamless, stylish, and durable. Begin by scuffing up the surface thoroughly so the concrete can get a better grip. Then apply a concrete topping mix or a homemade

A tile counter-
top reborn

batch of cement, fine sand, and acrylic or latex fortifier. Because the topping will be quite thin, you will need only relatively small batches. You'll need two or three layers.

To color the concrete, either incorporate pigment along with the other ingredients in at least the top coat, or apply stain at the end, as shown in this project.

DIRECTIONS

1 Remove switch plates and receptacle covers on the backsplash and cover the openings with blue painter's tape. Protect cabinets with plastic and the floor with kraft paper. Seal the doorway to other rooms, but open windows and any outside doors. Place a fan where it will push air through the room and outdoors. Put on goggles, ear protectors, heavy-duty gloves, and a respirator that protects against the tile dust you will stir up.

2 Holding a grinder at a 30-degree angle, rough up the surface of the tile.

3 With the claw end of a hammer, gouge corners and other spots that the grinder can't reach.

4 If you are preparing the concrete from scratch, select a measuring cup and mixing containers suitably sized to your project. A 1-pound coffee can—about 5½ cups—made a good measuring scoop for this 65-square-foot project, and 5-gallon buckets were perfect as mixing containers. Combine two scoops of cement and two scoops of 90-mesh sand in one mixing container. In the other, combine one scoop of water and one scoop of acrylic or latex fortifier. Add the dry ingredients to the liquid and mix for several minutes with a mixing paddle bit in an electric drill.

5 Put on rubber or latex gloves and spread the concrete over the backsplash with a cement finishing trowel. Work in 2- to 3-foot sections, trailing off the edges to avoid buildup where you stop and start. If the concrete is too thick and won't adhere to the backsplash, let the mixture rest in the bucket until it sets up a little—the concrete has an "open" (workable) time of approximately 15 minutes. If the mixture seems too thick at any time, use a spray bottle to apply a fine mist of water on the concrete. Make the surface as smooth as possible, but don't attempt to cover the tile or fill grout lines completely. This is merely a base coat.

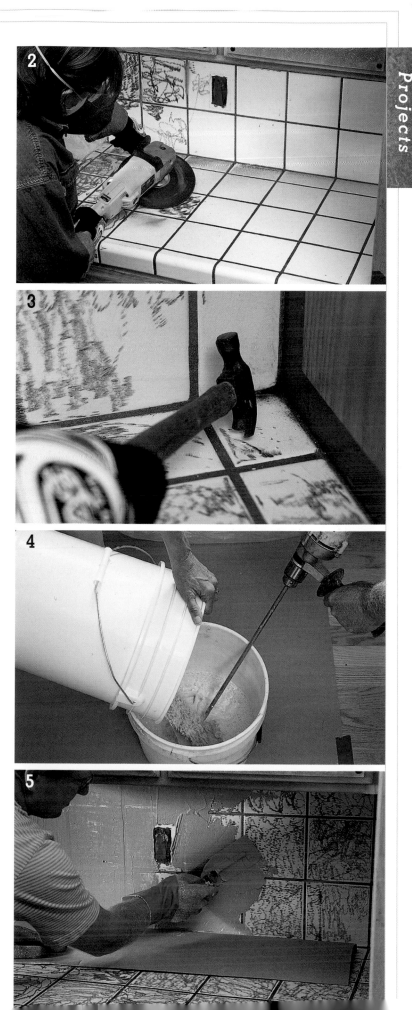

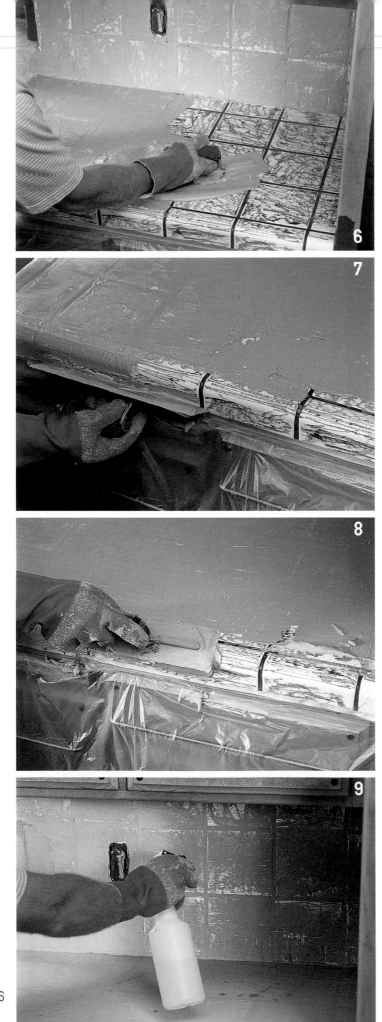

6 Trowel a base coat of concrete onto the countertop deck using the technique in Step 5.

7 To apply the concrete to the edge, load the trowel and hold it parallel to the countertop just below the lower edge of the tile trim, with the flat side of the trowel blade facing up.

8 Roll the trowel up and over the edge, coating the trim surface evenly. If your trim has a square edge, hold the trowel at an angle against the trim and drag the trowel upward without rolling it over the edge. The temperature and humidity will affect the drying time. Err on the side of safety and let the concrete dry overnight. Allow any leftover concrete to set up in the bucket until it's firm enough to hold together. Turn the bucket upside down to release the concrete and then break it apart to make it easier to dispose of.

9 Once the first coat is dry, put on a disposable respirator and sand down rough spots using 220-grit sandpaper. Clean off the sanding dust. Spray the surface with a fine mist of water in order to help the second coat adhere to the base coat.

10 Mix a second batch of concrete according to the instructions in Step 4. Trowel a second coat onto the backsplash as you did the first, working to cover the surface more completely this time. Trowel a second coat onto the countertop deck.

11 Trowel a second coat over the edge. To round the edge, use part of a plastic milk jug or a coffee can lid, bending and pulling it toward you as shown. The fortifier makes the mixture sticky, like white glue. If it seems too sticky and the plastic doesn't glide smoothly, spray the concrete with just enough water to give the surface a sheen and continue working. If the concrete is too wet, allow it to dry a little before continuing.

Allow the second coat to dry, then sand if needed. Apply a third coat to the backsplash, deck, and edge if needed. Allow to dry; sand.

12 If you wish to color the concrete with an acid stain, mix the concentrated stain with water in a glass container not used for food. Experiment on a scrap of dried concrete to find the stain-to-water ratio that you like. A ratio of 1 part stain to 10 parts water is used here. Don't be alarmed that the color of the stain is not what you expect. The stain reacts chemically with the cement to bring up the color.

Cover the deck with plastic and place a bucket of fresh water nearby. Put on rubber or latex gloves. With just a little stain on a paintbrush, apply it to the backsplash. Remove the plastic and apply the stain to the deck, then to the edging. Be sure not to drip on the surface, as drips can't be wiped up and will leave prominent, permanent marks. Have a helper work alongside you to wipe off excess stain with a tile sponge, rinsing the sponge often.

Wait for the period recommended by the manufacturer before you begin follow-up steps. You may need to neutralize the surface with baking soda and wipe down with a damp sponge to remove residue. Apply sealer to the backsplash and deck.

OPPOSITE: *Cast with a sinuous curve down the middle, this concrete sink is loaded with special features, including an integral drainboard and a metal grate that slides on a lip cast into the countertop. The basins have metal inlays on the bottom to guard against chipping. The metal is level with the surrounding concrete, so the surface is easy to clean.*

LEFT: *Dual sinks cast into a long countertop create a seamless surface that's easy to keep clean, while the matching multipart backsplash adds interesting detail in this bathroom. Because units such as this are almost always custom made, their dimensions can fit rooms precisely or accommodate existing plumbing.*

BELOW: *The essence of simplicity, this small vessel sink seems almost jadelike.*

BOTTOM: *Paired with a designer faucet styled to look like a bamboo fountain, this elegant vessel sink sets an Asian theme for this powder room.*

Sinks

LOOKING AS THOUGH THEY WERE CARVED FROM STONE, concrete sinks definitely make a design statement. That statement can range from high-style sleek to farmhouse practical, depending on the sink's style and surroundings. Because concrete has a tendency to chip when knocked with heavy pots, concrete sinks work best in powder rooms or other places where they aren't heavily used. They're also spectacular in outdoor kitchens, potting sheds, and the like, where a few chips just add to the rustic appeal. If you do opt for putting one in your kitchen, consider installing a metal inlay on the bottom in order to help absorb any blows.

ABOVE: *Angular and no-nonsense, a ramp sink and integral counter-top look high-tech and modern. Water drains through a slit at the bottom.*

LEFT: *With faucets at both ends, an unusually long bathroom sink offers all the advantages of the two-sink setup that's common in master bathrooms. But with this sink, you're never cramped. There is plenty of room to hand-wash delicate clothing or even to bathe a puppy.*

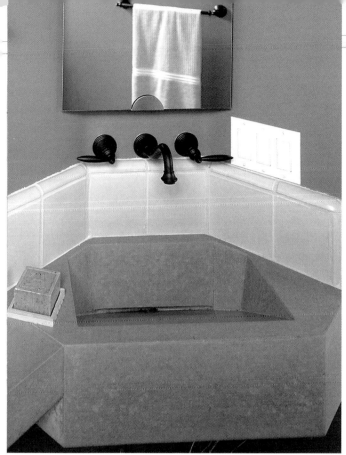

ABOVE, LEFT: *Snugged into a corner, this ramp sink joins with a slim counter to make the most efficient use possible of the tight space in a small bathroom. When concrete sinks and countertops are cast as one, they usually can be mounted to walls, creating a floating effect, or they can be attached to standard cabinet legs.*

ABOVE, RIGHT: *Known as a wave sink, this design merges sink and countertop and helps ensure that all the water goes down the drain. It's available with lots of waves—up to five sinks cast into a single countertop, a setup most in demand in commercial settings.*

RIGHT: *Cast into a countertop with a built-in drainboard, this sink pairs with a matching backsplash. To create the marbleized look, the manufacturer placed handfuls of sand mix into the mold, leaving slight gaps between clumps. Later, those gaps were plugged with a cement putty tinted a darker shade.*

121

Mantels, hearths, and fireplace surrounds

CONCRETE ABSORBS AND HOLDS HEAT but does not burn, making it a terrific material for mantels and fireplace surrounds. The flush-front gas and electric fireplaces common today sometimes seem like just part of the cabinetry, but with a concrete mantel or surround they become focal points. If you enjoy cozying up to a fire, consider adding an elevated hearth, which is also easy to execute in concrete. If you continue the hearth to a nearby wall, it will double as a seating ledge and a convenient place to set down books or trays of snacks.

BELOW: *A rough-hewn lintel made of natural stone contrasts with the smooth texture of the concrete surround and mantel.*

OPPOSITE, TOP: *Glazed tiles painted with an olive motif decorate this substantial fireplace surround, designed in a simple but classic style similar to that of fireplaces carved from stone.*

LEFT: *With its molded edge, this concrete mantel carries out the "European country" theme of the house. It also serves a practical purpose by wrapping around the corner to provide extra display space.*

BELOW: *When the fire's going, the raised hearth of this imposing fireplace becomes one of the coziest spots in the house. With a raised hearth, debris from a fire is less likely to spread across the floor, and you don't have to bend over as much to tend the fire.*

NEAR RIGHT: *Mitered like a picture frame, this fireplace surround helps create a somewhat formal tone in this room.*

FAR RIGHT: *This fireplace serves as a focal point in more ways than one. Above the concrete surround and mantel a television is tucked into a cabinet with doors that are normally kept closed.*

ABOVE: *This expansive hearth anchors an island wall that separates the living room from the music room. It also connects the fireplace and the wood storage area, provides spillover seating for guests, and works as a display area.*

RIGHT: *Although concrete surrounds often create a sense of mass, they also can look relatively petite, as this one does. It's important to match the size and style of a surround to the scale of the room.*

OPPOSITE, BOTTOM: *Similar in design to the fireplace shown at right, this surround nevertheless has a more massive look. The firebox is elevated and the mantel is thicker.*

129

Floors

NOT TOO LONG AGO, IF YOU HAD A CONCRETE FLOOR, chances are you covered it up with tile, linoleum, carpet, or wood—anything to hide that ugly gray. That's no longer the case. Today, thanks to acid stains, paints, stamps, and other products, as well as a growing awareness of how to use them, concrete floors can be works of art. If you're planning a new house or an addition, choosing a decorative concrete floor will probably save you money because you won't need any other finished flooring. If you have an existing house, a wide array of topping mixtures, some of which need to be only $\frac{1}{8}$ inch thick, allow you to create a decorative concrete floor over whatever subfloor you have.

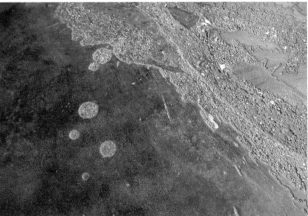

132

ABOVE: *Bathed in sunlight, the concrete here not only serves as functional, beautiful flooring; it also helps heat the house. Concrete is an ideal flooring in passive-solar houses because it absorbs and holds onto heat that the sun provides during the day. The concrete then releases that stored energy as the room temperature cools down in the evening.*

RIGHT: *Johnny Grey, a kitchen designer from England, included Chippendale-style cabinets and sweeping curves in this kitchen. Custom-made cement-body floor tiles in contrasting colors and shapes add to the distinctive look. The tiles, each up to 30 inches square, look a bit like marble because of the way the concrete was placed into the molds a handful at a time.*

OPPOSITE, TOP: *A concrete floor pulls together the elements of this easy-care living room, which also features a built-in concrete bench, a concrete fireplace surround, and a concrete coffee table. They contrast beautifully with the bright walls and the glowing amber of natural wood.*

OPPOSITE, MIDDLE: *Aiming to mimic the look of a beach, the contractor who created this unusual floor incorporated aquarium sands and seashells. He also applied several colors of acid stains.*

OPPOSITE, BOTTOM: *Buff and copper acid stains create the mottled color on this floor.*

ABOVE, LEFT: *Because pigments that stand up to the alkalinity of cement tend to be somewhat muted and the designers of this floor wanted vivid color, they opted to paint the design. Water-based paints work best for painting floors.*

ABOVE, RIGHT: *A ⅛-inch layer of gray polymer-modified concrete was applied over an old concrete floor. The next day, acid stain in a color known as Aged Buff was rubbed in. Two coats of sealer and two of wax produced the sheen.*

OPPOSITE: *Thinned, naturally pigmented linseed oil–based paints add a warm look to this concrete floor.*

BELOW, RIGHT: *This floor was topped with a cement-acrylic mixture, then troweled and burnished. Powdered mica was scattered on the topping as it was being troweled.*

BELOW: *Looking very much like handmade Saltillo tiles, the main expanse of this concrete floor was created by cutting a grid and staining the squares with several tones of acid stain. After the stain dried, the grid lines were filled with grout.*

Most of the concrete floors shown in this book were poured when the house was built. But it's possible to create similar designs on existing floors by using a cementitious coating. Some manufacturers recommend using their toppings only over concrete sub-floors, but the product we chose, Rotofino, from Colormaker Floors, can also be used over wood subfloors. The trick is to first install a layer of ½-inch HardiePlank™, a type of cement board, which stiffens the floor and provides a cement-based sub-strate so the coating can bond properly. Taping the joints should prevent gaps between the cement board from showing in the finished floor, but you may still want to design your floor with lines that follow these joints. That way, if cracks do develop, they will look like part of your design.

A decorative cement floor topping

DIRECTIONS

1 Assemble the needed tools: a ½-inch drill (can be rented) with a paddle mixer and a 5-gallon bucket; homemade knee boards (shown) with only screw tips protruding on the back so that you can work on the coating to trowel it; a floor gauge roller with ¹⁄₁₆-inch-deep ridges; and a pool trowel, which has rounded ends.

2 Screw ½-inch-thick HardiePlank™ panels to the subfloor, using one screw at each mark on the panel. Cover seams with mesh tape and trowel a thinset mortar (we used Slimpatch™ from the L. M. Scofield Company) over the tape, as if you were covering joints in drywall.

3 The next day, when the patches are dry, use a garden sprayer to apply the primer, as recommended by the manufacturer. Use two coats if that is recommended.

4 Prepare the coating as the label specifies. Working from a back corner toward a doorway in sections small enough so that you can reach across them, pour on a few cupfuls of the coating and immediately smooth out the product with the floor gauge roller. Work quickly.

5 Allow the coating to stiffen, then trowel smooth with the pool trowel. Work on the knee boards, smoothing over your tracks as you back out of the room.

6 The next day, decorate the coating. Score a grid with an angle grinder (wear a mask and goggles), then mist on two coats of acid stain. Rub in the first coat with a sponge and the second with a rag. Acid stains look clear at first. The color develops over an hour or so.

7 Neutralize the acid with an alkali as the manufacturer recommends. Rinse with water a few times and remove with a shop vac until the water is clear. Allow to dry. Seal and wax.

Paths and patios

CONCRETE PATHS AND PATIOS often mimic natural stone. They can also have a look all their own. Consider finishes used on interior floors, provided the surfaces aren't too slick. Or opt for treatments, such as exposed aggregate, that typically are used only outdoors.

Big expanses of paving are probably best left to professionals, but smaller-scale paths or patios make good projects for people with only a little experience building with concrete. The smaller the pour, the better. If this is your introduction to this material, a project such as the steppingstone path, on page 142, is an ideal place to start.

OPPOSITE, TOP: *Large, individually cast pavers create an inviting courtyard that looks striking because of the interplay of stone sizes. To create a project like this without having to lift the heavy pavers, pour alternate sections and then fill in between them, as shown in the project that begins on page 146.*

OPPOSITE, MIDDLE: *Like a carpet under a dining table, a grid of rectangles and diamonds sets off this patio dining area.*

OPPOSITE, BOTTOM: *This used to be an old, cracked concrete driveway. Using a 4-inch angle grinder, a concrete artist first cut random lines, then applied acid stains.*

RIGHT: *Contractors who specialize in decorative concrete use pigments and either stamps or paper stencils with textured rollers to produce surfaces that resemble slate or other stone.*

BELOW: *This pathway and driveway started out as ordinary concrete. A topping of polymer concrete was added and the flagstone design was stamped in.*

ABOVE: *Smooth concrete tinted with several tones of acid stains enrich this walkway and patio. The ball decorations along the edges are also made of concrete and were cast in molds sold for this purpose.*

LEFT: *Pillow-shaped concrete pavers tinted in slightly different shades help give this California patio an Old World look. The owner devised the technique as a less expensive alternative to importing stone paving from Europe.*

OPPOSITE, TOP: *Diamond-shape pavers create a fun harlequin look at this urban residence.*

OPPOSITE, BOTTOM: *The builders of this house have Italian roots and love Italian architecture, so they tried to incorporate key features in the design of this New World home. A bare concrete patio just would not do; they outlined borders by cutting around the edge and the center. Then they colored the design with acid stains and added a birdbath to complete the look.*

By casting individual steppingstones, you can create a one-of-a-kind pathway without having to deal with a large quantity of concrete all at once. Each concrete batch is small, so you should have plenty of time to add pebble mosaics or other decorations, even if you work alone.

A steppingstone path

Although the shape of these steppingstones is complex, the mold is easy to build. Create the curved shape by cutting a plywood base and then attaching strips of aluminum or galvanized-steel flashing around the edges. We used a kidney shape, so the back of one piece interlocks with the front of the next piece. This allows you to place the steppingstones close together to create a solid walkway if you wish.

With our shape, one 60-pound bag of sand mix was more than enough to fill the mold. We measured the amount left over and reduced the dry ingredients by a little less than that on subsequent pours.

DIRECTIONS

1 Sketch the shape on newspaper and transfer it to ¾-inch plywood. Our design is 25 inches long and about 14 inches wide. Cut along the line with a jigsaw.

2 For a mold 2 inches deep, cut aluminum or galvanized-steel flashing into a strip 2¾ inches wide and long enough to go around the mold with a little excess. (Measure the perimeter with string.) To cut the metal without creating ripples, score it several times with a utility knife. Then fold the sheet back and forth against a straightedge. If the flashing is thin, cut two strips and sandwich them together with plastic tape, as we did. Nail the bottom of the strip or strips to the plywood; use screws on inward curves so you can release the edging later.

3 Spray the base with shellac to reduce the amount of moisture the plywood will absorb. When the shellac dries, spray all interior mold surfaces with cooking oil. Blot with a paper towel. Screw short pieces of wood to the ends of the form so you have handles to help you remove the mold.

Tip

YOU CAN ALSO USE THIS TECHNIQUE to build molds for counter-tops, tabletops, and other curved projects.

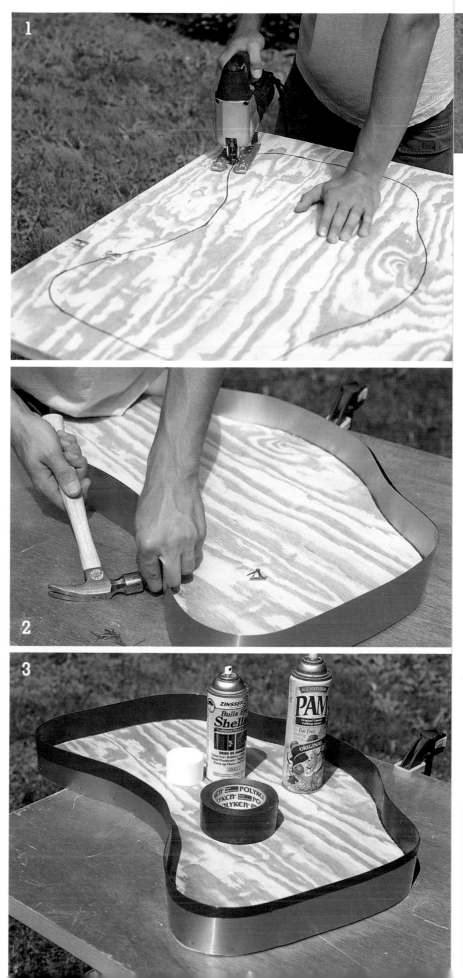

4 Prepare Basic Sand Mix, page 52, or a bagged sand mix. Fill the mold with it. Begin decorating immediately. Outline shapes, if you wish, by lightly pressing cookie cutter patterns made of flashing into the surface. Dampen pebbles and place them into the sand mix vertically. Submerge most of each piece. As you complete a section, cover the stones with a small piece of plywood and, using a hammer, tamp them nearly flush with the surface. If your design includes large and small stones, place and tamp large ones first; then add the small pieces and tamp again.

5 With a trowel, embed all the stones securely by working the surface cream of cement and fine sand between the pieces. It's fine to cover the stones completely with the sand mix.

6 Wait several hours, until the sand mix stiffens. Then brush off the surface to reveal the pebbles. If the concrete is still rather soft, use a nylon brush and wipe the surface with a sponge that's been well wrung out. If the concrete is hard, use a metal brush and rinse with a fine spray of water.

7 In one to two days, remove the steppingstone from the mold. Loosen screws on inward curves and break the seal around the top edge with a putty knife. Invert, resting the handles on scraps of wood so the steppingstone can drop out. If gravity isn't enough, tap the form with a mallet.

8 Round over the edge with a stiff, sharp-edged tool. A painter's 5-in-1 tool works well.

9 Establish the route of your path with a hose, then set steppingstones in place. If you want them one stride apart, walk across the lawn and mark your footprints. Or establish a set stride length and subtract the width of one steppingstone. Cut a spacer block to match the remaining distances. Our pieces are 8 inches apart.

10 To set a steppingstone into a lawn without creating a mess, hammer a 2-inch-wide brick chisel straight down around the edge of the concrete. Remove the steppingstone and use gloved hands or a small shovel to separate the root mat from the underlying soil. Roll back the sod and remove.

11 Smooth a layer of sand across the hole, then tip the steppingstone into place. Jiggle it back and forth until it feels level and solid.

Tip

IF A STEPPINGSTONE STILL WOBBLES after you set it on sand, remove the piece, take out a handful of sand at the center of the hole, and replace the steppingstone. Press and wiggle it until you have seated it firmly.

Pouring a path in place allows you to build a wide expanse of weed-free paving without having to carry or level the finished pieces. This pathway was designed for a family that wanted a folk theme. Because they raise chickens, the design evolved to include feather inlays (cut from copper) and a texture created by pressing chicken wire into the surface as it stiffened.

A path that's poured in place

This 4-inch-thick path is 9½ feet long and varies in width from 2 feet to 6½ feet, too small to have concrete delivered from a truck and too large for a few people to mix and pour concrete all at once. So the path was poured in stages: first the ends, then the middle. We used a 3.5-cubic-foot mixer, sold at home centers.

DIRECTIONS

1 Excavate the area, spread gravel, and build a form, as shown on page 40. Tamp the gravel base thoroughly. Use a motorized tamper (before you add the forms) if you have a large space or a hand tamper, as shown here, if you have a small space.

2 With aviator's snips or another suitable tool, cut pieces of chicken wire to fit within each section, minus a 2-inch perimeter. Remove the wire and place it on the lawn or on another flat area. Weight the wire so it straightens.

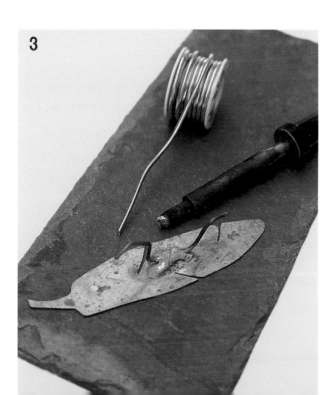

3 Make feather inlays or other designs from copper sheeting, which cuts almost as easily as wood. Wearing goggles, use a scroll saw or a coping saw with a fine-tooth blade. File edges. Solder wire strands to the backs to anchor the inlays to the concrete. Clean off flux residue.

Tip

YOU CAN ALSO CREATE a patio using this method. Build forms in a checkerboard and pour alternate sections. Then go back and pour the rest. If you use rot-resistant material for the forms, you can leave them in place as part of your design.

4 Prepare Basic Concrete Mix, page 52, or a bagged mix (with ½ gallon extra cement per bag if you use a standard mix). You'll need several batches to fill each section of a path this size. Dump each batch into the form and spread with a shovel. Tamp thoroughly when the section is full.

5 Run a straight 2 by 4 back and forth across the form to screed, or level, the concrete.

6 Run an edging tool around the perimeter. If rocks get in the way, first smooth the edge by pressing straight down with a margin trowel. Don't attempt to make the edge perfectly smooth at this point; your main goal is to push down any rocks that are near the surface.

7 Allow the concrete to set a little. Then smooth the section with a trowel.

8 Embed the feather inlays. Press them down into the concrete and wiggle them gently to help the concrete fill in around the anchor wires. It's better to seat inlays a bit too deep than to risk having them sit above the surface, where an edge might lift up.

9 When the surface is somewhat stiff but still pliable, carefully set the chicken wire in place. With a trowel in each hand, transfer the design by pressing straight down. Vary the pressure if you want a variegated surface, as we did. Don't attempt to trowel in a circular motion; your tool will snag on the wire. Lift the wire and smooth the perimeter with the edging tool again.

10 As the concrete hardens, clean excess concrete from the inlay surface with a sponge.

11 Keep the concrete damp for at least three days. Then remove the perimeter forms.

Tip

TO KEEP CONCRETE damp in dry weather, cover it with plastic or cardboard and mist it several times a day. Or apply a curing compound. Pigment manufacturers recommend using these compounds on tinted concrete to prevent stains that can appear if the concrete dries unevenly.

Furniture

CONCRETE FURNITURE RANGES from simple benches and tabletops to complex barbecue setups. In a sunroom or family room, a tabletop made of concrete sets the tone for casual elegance. Outdoors, concrete benches, chairs, and tables serve double duty, providing both practicality and garden decoration. The concrete gradually weathers to resemble valuable antiques carved from stone.

There are several practical details to deal with before you buy or build concrete furniture. First, consider the weight. A concrete tabletop will need to remain where you install it. So will concrete seating, unless it's made from special lightweight mixes. A firm footing, such as a poured concrete pad, is needed for outdoor tables or heavy pedestals so they don't sink or tip. And remember that concrete benches can be hard. Provide cushions if you want your guests to linger.

ABOVE: *A polished slab of concrete made with bits of recycled Chardonnay bottles as the aggregate serves as an easy-care tabletop in this dining room.*

OPPOSITE, BOTTOM: *The glass top on this table invites visitors to contemplate the forces that hold together parts of the base, which is made of a lightweight concrete called Syndesis.*

BELOW: *This three-piece lounging bench interlocks in a way that helps keep the pieces aligned.*

NEAR RIGHT: *Mounted to a wall, a simple box made of concrete works well in an entry as a catchall for wet umbrellas, keys, and other items.*

FAR RIGHT: *Made from lightweight Syndesis concrete, this table and bench add to the easygoing ambiance of a dining area. The floor is also concrete, so the benches slide easily when it's time to clean up.*

FAR LEFT: *Cast upside down in a mold, this desktop looks striking in part because of its intricate edge pattern. Creating the mold for the design was easy: the builder merely tacked wood molding into the form walls.*

NEAR LEFT: *Pieces of broken pottery inlay the edges of this 16-foot-long concrete table, set in a garden filled with artistic touches brought back from the designer's global travels. The table seats 12 but is often used as a roomy buffet table.*

OPPOSITE, TOP: *Concrete furniture isn't something you move around on a whim. It tends to stay where it is—like this table, which was built to encircle the tree at the center.*

RIGHT: *In a house with concrete floors, this concrete table fits right in. It's used for everything from paying bills to eating a quick meal.*

BELOW: *This free-form mosaic tabletop reflects the sunny mood of the rest of the well-lighted room. An artist glued broken pieces of tile to a base surrounded by a metal band and then filled in around the tiles with a concrete patch product usually used to fill cracks in driveways.*

Created in three parts, this garden bench is spacious enough for two people to share a view or pause to chat. The seat, cast with two recesses underneath, slips into place over rebar stubs that protrude from the legs. Both the seat and the legs include decora-

A garden bench

tive features. The top was lightly dusted with white cement and then colored with two tones of acid stain, Padre Brown and Antique Bronze. That produced a richly aged look. The edges are ragged, reminiscent of rough-hewn stone, but the top edge is rounded over for comfort. The legs boast a rippled edge, created by slipping short pieces of metal roofing into the form.

DIRECTIONS

1 Create a decorative edge for the legs with strips of metal roofing. Cut two pieces 6 inches wide using a circular saw with a metal roofing blade or a plywood blade attached backward. To guide the saw, screw a straightedge to plywood and clamp this assembly over the roofing, which should be supported with pieces of 2 by 4 on sawhorses. Wear goggles and ear protection—you'll see sparks and hear a screech.

2 Build the form for the legs. Draw a cut-off triangle on a 2-foot-square piece of melamine-coated particleboard. Our shape is 16 inches high, 15 inches wide at the base, and 7 inches wide at the top. Extend lines around to the back so you know where to locate screws. Cut edge pieces 6 inches wide and bevel the ends to match your drawing. Cut the top and bottom pieces so they reach past the sides. In the top piece, drill a $\frac{1}{2}$-inch hole, centered. Screw the sides to the base and then screw the top and bottom to the sides. With tin snips, cut the roofing strips to fit. Slide them into place.

3 Spray the interior with cooking oil. Prepare Basic Concrete Mix, page 52, or a bagged mix (with $\frac{1}{2}$ gallon extra cement if you use a standard mix). One 80-pound bag of high-strength concrete mix was the perfect amount. Fill the form halfway. Mark a 6-inch stub of rebar $\frac{5}{8}$ inch from one end with easy-to-see blue painter's tape. Slip the rebar through the hole in the top and adjust the bar so the mark lines up with the inside of the form. Finish filling the form and trowel the surface smooth. After a day or two, unscrew the top and bottom and tip the concrete out of the form. Pull off the metal, clean the form of excess concrete, and spray the mold with cooking oil before refilling for the second leg.

4 Cut pieces for the bench-seat form by making an open box from melamine-coated particleboard. Our base is 15 inches wide and 48 inches long, ringed by sidepieces that are 3¼ inches wide (to produce a seat 2½ inches thick).

5 Line the sidepieces with potter's clay before you attach them to the base. Slice off pieces of clay with wire and roll flat. Cut off a ¾-inch-wide strip along one edge so the base piece can slide underneath.

6 Screw the sides to the base and to each other at the corners. Press a broken brick into the clay, working your way around the form. Then, with a potter's cutting tool, carve a rounded edge into the clay along the base. This creates the mold for a snag-free edge along the top of the seat.

7 Spray the clay with cooking oil and lightly mist oil onto the base of the mold. Wipe all the excess from the melamine. If you wish, sift a few drifts of white cement over the bottom of the mold. This will create a "Milky Way" look on the final piece. Or, if you coat the concrete with acid stains, as we did, it will add to the color variation.

Tip

IF YOU CONSTRUCT a one-person bench, about 30 inches long, you can omit the rebar.

8 Prepare another batch of concrete mix to fill the bench-top form. Add mix one handful at a time, creating a layer about ½ inch thick. Tamp out air bubbles. With a hammer, beat on the form from underneath. You should see bubbles rise. Stop when a water glaze covers the surface.

9 Continue filling the form, stopping periodically to tap the sides with a hammer. When the form is full and you're finished tapping, level the surface with a 2 by 4. Place three pieces of ⅜-inch rebar lengthwise, 1 inch from each side and down the middle. Tap them down as shown on page 159. Smooth over the surface with a trowel. To create recesses to hold the rebar stubs on the legs, fill two pipe caps with clay and stick them to pieces of plastic. Wiggle the caps down into the concrete about 9 inches from each end, keeping the plastic flush with the surface.

10 Cover and allow to cure for at least two days, then remove the form and plastic over the pipe caps. Fill any holes with a paste of cement, pigment, and water. Allow the seat to dry slowly in shade.

11 When the seat is at least two weeks old, apply acid stain. Follow the manufacturer's safety instructions. Brush on the watery solution and wait for vivid color to develop. Neutralize remaining stain with baking soda. Scrub away residue with handfuls of sawdust. Rinse thoroughly.

157

With a few simple adjustments, you can turn the bench project on page 154 into one that results in a table. The legs are the same as those for the bench, except that you need four and must cast a length of pipe down the middle of each one, rather than

A concrete table

insert the rebar stub. When you have made all the parts, you can invert two legs on top of the others, thread rebar through the pipes to pin the leg pieces together, and, presto, the bench structure rises to table height. A nub of rebar that protrudes from each leg holds the tabletop in place.

We cast the top right side up and troweled the surface smooth before pressing on vine maple leaves dusted with pigment and cement. This table is heavy. Make sure you have a stable base.

DIRECTIONS

1 Build a leg form like the one on page 155, but drill ⅝-inch holes in the top and bottom for a dowel that temporarily holds up a ½-inch plastic pipe cut to the leg's height. Copying the bench leg exactly results in a table 32½ inches high—4 inches taller than most dining tables but a good height for a potting bench or other work surface. Adjust the height if you wish.

2 Build an open box to mold the tabletop. Ours is 24 inches wide and 49 inches long. The mold sides are 3¼ inches deep, producing a top 2½ inches thick. For a shaped edge, nail mitered molding to the sides. Create recesses for the rebar, as shown in Step 9 on page 157. Prepare Basic Concrete Mix, page 52, or a bagged concrete mix (with ½ gallon extra cement if you use a standard mix). Pour the concrete, pound under and around the form with a hammer, and screed the surface. Then place four pieces of ⅜-inch-thick rebar (cut 2 inches shorter than the top) onto the concrete. Equally space the pieces, starting 1 inch from the sides. With a marked stick and a hammer, tap the rebar 1 inch deep. Smooth the surface with a trowel. Slightly round over the outer edge with a trowel.

3 Decorate the concrete after all surface water is gone. Mist the veined side of leaves with water. Dust with a mixture of pigment and cement. Place the leaves, pigment side down, on the concrete. Smooth edges so the leaves adhere. Carefully trowel over them. Wipe the trowel if it picks up pigment. Then trowel the entire tabletop again. Cover. Peel off the leaves when the concrete is firm. Remove edge forms after about two days. Keep the concrete damp for several more days before you put the table together.

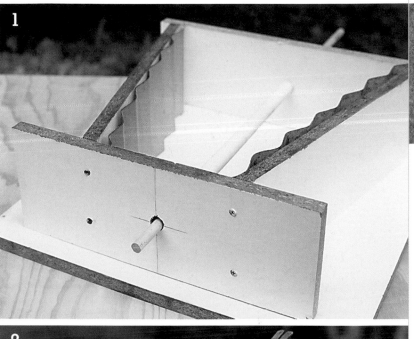

With the elegant look of marble, this surface is surprisingly easy to make. It is actually easier than a single-color tabletop because the marbling technique eliminates concerns about air bubbles.

A tabletop with a marble-like surface

To create the marbled look, first press a stiff sand-and-cement mixture against a mold one handful at a time. This leaves small gaps between the additions, which you later fill with a cement mixture tinted in the same or a contrasting color. Even if you use the same pigment, the colors will come out slightly different because the moisture and aggregate content of the patch differs from that of the main batch. This creates a subtle marble effect.

Marble effects work well on many projects, including fireplace surrounds and garden pots. However, it's possible only when objects are cast upside down or inside out in a mold. Right-side-up objects need to be troweled, which would cover up the gaps that look like veins.

DIRECTIONS

1 Build the basic form by screwing 2½-inch-wide strips of ¾-inch-thick melamine-coated particleboard to a base piece of the same material. The space in the middle determines the table's dimensions. This one is 52 inches long and 32 inches wide. To give the table a thick look but keep weight down, screw 1-inch-wide spacers (cut from the particleboard material) to the top edge of each sidepiece.

2 Build a screed, or leveling board, that you can use to hollow out the center of the table. From plywood at least ½ inch thick, cut one strip about 6 inches longer than the table's width. Cut a second, deeper piece about 8 inches shorter than the table's width. Screw the two pieces together so the deeper piece drops down and leaves a 1½-inch gap at the bottom. Using a spacer underneath makes this step easier.

3 Cut reinforcement so there is a 1-inch gap around the edges, then remove it and set it aside. Ladder wire is used here.

4 Coat the mold with a thin layer of form-release material. Use a product made for this purpose or improvise with cooking oil. Wipe off any puddles.

5 Prepare Basic Sand Mix (page 52) or a bagged sand mix. Whether you mix by machine or by hand, add just enough liquid to make a very stiff mix that keeps its shape. There should be little or no slump (see page 63).

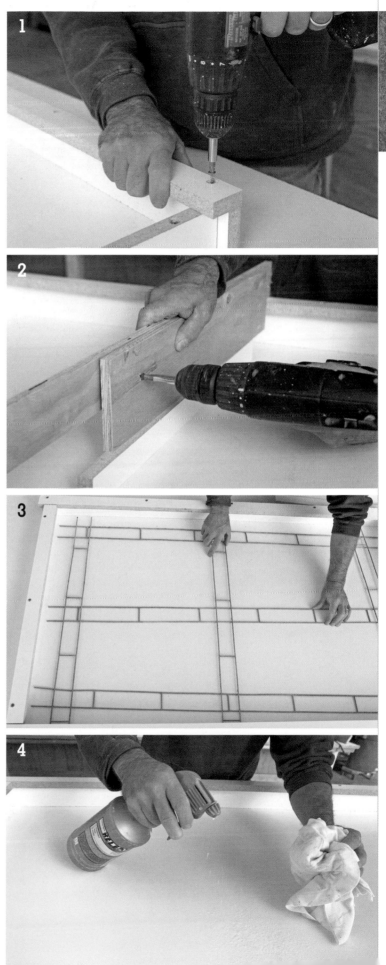

6 One handful at a time, pat the mixture into the mold. Press it all the way up the sides but only about ¾ inch deep in the center. Pack the concrete particularly well along the top and bottom edges of the sides.

7 Place the reinforcement onto the concrete. Keep it 1 inch from all exterior edges. Overlap pieces where necessary. You don't need to tie them together. As extra insurance against cracks, mix polypropylene fibers into the remaining concrete (see page 48). Then add another layer of concrete about ¾ inch thick. Completely fill areas tucked under the edge spacers.

8 Using the screed you made in step 2, smooth the center of the table and create a crisp 90-degree angle along each thick edge. Stop screeding when the surface is level. It doesn't need to be smooth.

9 Wait one hour, then go over the surface with a wooden float. If you see holes, fill them in with a little of the leftover concrete mixture.

10 Cover the mold with plastic and wait until the next day.

11 Remove the screws holding the mold sides in place. With a helper, slide the tabletop just far enough off one edge of your worktable so you can grip it. Pivot the piece upward. When it's balanced on one edge, one person can let go, walk around to the other side, and slide four pairs of short 2 by 4s out as spacers. Then lower the tabletop onto the blocks.

12 Now the fun of marbleizing begins. Where you see light-colored lines, only a thin layer of cement covers gaps. Use a wire brush to remove this layer and expose the gaps. Sweep away the debris with a soft-bristle brush.

13 Prepare a slurry of cement, pigment, and acrylic or latex fortifier, or use a mix sold for this purpose. It should have the consistency of yogurt. With a wide putty knife, work the material into the gaps as if you were cleaning a window with a squeegee. It's fine to leave some gaps.

14 Wait an hour or so. As the first slurry coat dries, it will shrink slightly. Mix up a second batch, perhaps in a different color, and go over the table again. Wait an hour and repeat until the slurry no longer leaves divots as it dries. Then mist the table-top with water and cover it with plastic.

15 The next day, move the table to a place where spilled water won't be a problem. Keep the surface damp while you sand off the surface slurry. Use a stone polisher with a diamond pad, or use a hand diamond pad. Start with 200-grit, then 400, and work your way up to 3,000 if you wish. Hand pads work best on edges and corners. Allow the table to dry, then apply a penetrating sealer, followed by a topical sealer.

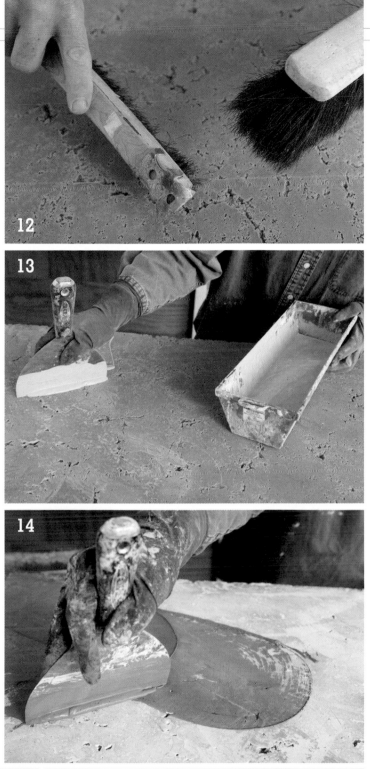

Planters

BELOW: *Circular concrete shapes resist cracking better than square shapes do, an important consideration if you live where winter temperatures drop below freezing and you plan to keep a planter outdoors all year. Many different shapes qualify as "circular," as this picture shows.*

CONCRETE PLANTERS range from petite pieces perfect for a single orchid to giant urns capable of housing trees. There are several construction methods, shown in the following projects. Some concrete planters stand up to freezing weather while others fall apart as ice crystals form and cause the concrete to crack. The key is the amount of water used in the initial mix. If you add only enough so the cement mixture barely clumps into a ball, the planter should survive in all weather conditions. The pressed pot on page 166 depends on this technique. You can also use this approach for the carved pot (page 172) and the tufa planter (page 168).

OPPOSITE, TOP: *As concrete planters age, some of the surface cream of cement and fine sand erodes, exposing larger grains of sand in the mix. This just adds to the rustic appeal of the pots.*

ABOVE, LEFT: *Although the pot is concrete and the post underneath is natural stone, they pair beautifully, especially because of their lichen glaze.*

ABOVE, RIGHT: *Adding artistic elements made of concrete is a great way to turn a garden into a personal retreat. In this garden, the owner placed a large water bowl at the center and added statuary and other garden art around it.*

RIGHT: *Created with layers of colored concrete, this tall planter and base add a sense of height to a garden.*

Create garden pots that rival expensive European antiques by using a round rock to pound a mixture of cement and sand into a sturdy form. Known as "dry-casting," this technique depends on adding only the minimum amount of water. You need to be able

A pressed pot

to get the mixture to clump, but it cannot sag out of shape. Pounding the mixture into the form produces a glorious surface on the molded face, one more like sandstone than concrete. Because the cement never gets wet enough to create a paste, there's little point in adding pigment to this type of project. The sand color predominates. It's worth searching out tan or yellow sand to give your pots a special look. Even fine details of the mold transfer beautifully. Planters made this way are quite porous. Put plants in a plastic pot and set that into the concrete planter.

DIRECTIONS

1 Find or build a mold to support the exterior of your planter. If the mold flexes, embed it in sand. We used a 20-inch-wide plastic garden pot and filled part of the base ring with plasticine clay so remaining sections would become feet on the finished pot. For a drain hole, screw through the mold into a short piece of dowel on the interior. Spray with cooking oil and wipe off the excess.

2 Wearing a mask and gloves, combine 2 parts sand and 1 part cement. Incorporate plastic fibers (sold as reinforcing for concrete) if you wish. Work in just enough water so you can squeeze the mixture into a ball. Starting at the bottom, pound handfuls against the mold with a round rock. Aim for a layer about 1 inch thick. For especially large pots, walls can be up to 2 inches thick. Cover the pot and keep it moist.

3 Free the bowl from the mold after two days. Invert the mold and unscrew the drain dowel. Tap the mold with a mallet to free the pot. You may have to hit the mold rather aggressively; aim for the base, not the walls. Remove the drain dowel by drilling through it with an undersize bit; pick out remaining wood with pliers.

4 If the top edge looks ragged, smooth it with a rasp and a sanding sponge. Smooth the interior, if necessary, with the sanding sponge, scrapers, or other tools.

Incorporate peat moss in a mixture of sand and cement and you'll wind up with "hypertufa," a rocklike material that resembles natural tufa stone. Pronounced "toofa," it often develops a crust of moss and lichen, adding to its appeal. Hypertufa planters make ideal troughs for miniature alpine plants or cacti. Because a rustic appearance is part of the charm, forms for shaping hypertufa can be supersimple. You can use nesting cardboard boxes or mold the material freehand on the outside of an old plastic pot. After several days, the mixture will be hard enough for you to fine-tune the shape with a wire brush or improvised carving tools. Allow hypertufa pots to cure out of direct sunlight for several weeks.

A hypertufa planter

DIRECTIONS

1 Nesting cardboard boxes with a gap of at least 1 inch all around make good molds. Brace the sides with concrete blocks or wood clamped in place. If one box is more rectangular than the other, you can adjust the larger box by screwing pieces of wood inside. We added wood to only the lower portion of opposite walls to create handles. If you want a drain hole, tape a short dowel or a pipe stub to the bottom of the box and oil it well.

2 There are several recipes for hypertufa. A basic one: mix 2 parts sand and 2 parts sifted peat moss with 1 to 1½ cups cement. Or, for a more lightweight mix, substitute perlite (the white component in this mortar tray) for half of the sand. Combine dry ingredients, then add enough water to make a moist but not soggy mix that you can form into clumps.

3 Set the large box on a flat surface where it can remain undisturbed for several days. Fill the bottom with the cement mixture and pack it firmly. Stop when the bottom is as thick as the gap between the two boxes. Insert the smaller box and fill with bags of sand. Press the cement mixture between the walls, tamping as you go. Round over the top edge. Cover with plastic.

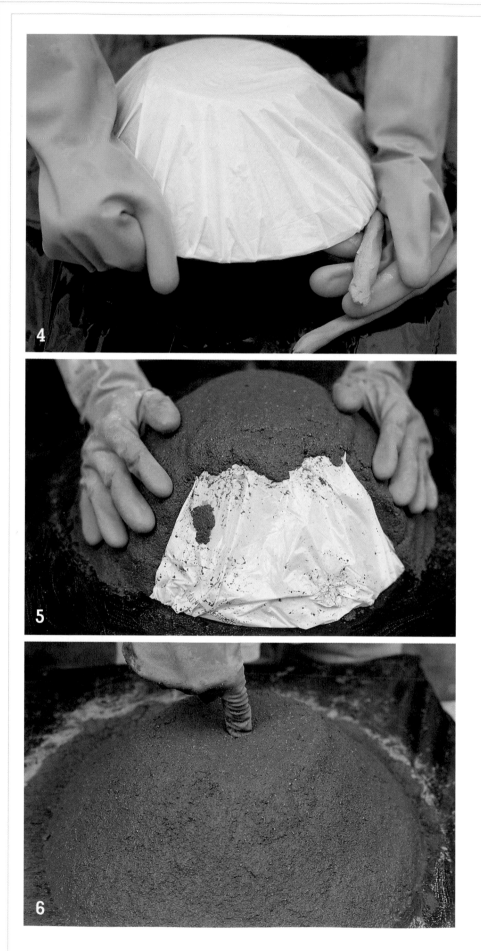

4 Instead of forming hypertufa between two cardboard boxes, you can use a smooth bowl as a form and apply the material by hand to its exterior. Slip a thin plastic bag over the bowl first to make the cast easy to remove. Spread out the plastic and invert the bowl over a sturdy surface where your project can remain undisturbed for several days. Attach the bowl to the work surface with a pad of potter's clay, if you have one.

5 Mix the hypertufa using one of the recipes in Step 2 on page 169. Keep the mixture stiff; add only enough water so you can press the tufa into a ball. Form hamburger-size patties and pat them onto the bowl, aiming for a layer about 1 inch thick. Start at the rim and work up.

6 Shape what will be the bottom of the planter into a concave curve so the pot won't wobble. If you want a drain hole, poke it in now.

Tip

TO NEUTRALIZE THE ALKALINITY of the cement before you plant, immerse your pot in a solution of ½ cup vinegar to 1 gallon water for about a half hour. To hasten the growth of moss and algae on the planter, paint it with a mixture of beer and sugar or a mix of butter-milk and pulverized moss.

7 Whether you have shaped your tufa planter with cardboard boxes or with a plastic-covered bowl, wait at least 1½ days for the mixture to firm up; then remove the mold. (If you screwed wood to the cardboard, remove the screws before you pull away the box.)

8 With a wire brush or a rasp, fine-tune the shape and remove telltale signs of the mold, such as ribs from corrugated cardboard or wrinkles from plastic. Because tufa planters are meant to resemble weathered rock, they usually look best with a rough surface. Although the tufa is stiff at this point, it is still rather weak. Handle your planter carefully.

9 You can carve details into your tufa planter if you wish. Consider Mayan designs and other ancient artwork that was executed by chipping into rock. As with any project made with cement, the longer you keep your planter damp, the stronger it will become. Keep it covered for at least several more days and out of the sun for several weeks.

171

It's very easy to carve cement mixtures when they are set but not yet very strong. If you try to remove a garden pot from a typical mold at this point, however, the bowl is likely to crumble. This project features a mold system that's easy to remove so you can

A carved pot

begin carving as soon as possible. The mold consists of a circular base plus inner and outer rings made of metal flashing. You tamp a sand-cement mixture over the bottom and up the sides, wait for the mix to stiffen, and remove the outside ring. Leaving the pot on its base, you can then begin carving.

DIRECTIONS

1 With a jigsaw or a band saw, cut a circular base from ³/₄-inch-thick plywood or melamine-coated particleboard. For a drain hole, screw through the base into a dowel stub. Cut two lengths of metal flashing to go around the base, plus a little extra. Fit one around the base, tie string to hold the shape, and screw the flashing in place. Tape the overlapped top edge and the outside free end. Form the other piece into a smaller ring. Establish the size by using a thick dowel (about 1¼ inches wide) as a spacer inside the bigger ring. Tie string, then tape the top overlap and the interior free end, and remove the string. Spray the interior with cooking oil.

2 Prepare Basic Sand Mix, page 52, or a bagged sand mix with a minimum amount of water. Pack the mixture into the bottom of the form, then insert the smaller ring and stiffen it by filling the center with bags of sand. Continue filling the form, packing as you go with the same dowel that you used to size the inner ring.

3 After several hours, when the concrete has set, you can begin carving. First, remove screws around the base and cut or peel off tape on the outside ring. You can leave the inner ring in place or remove it by first lifting out the bags of sand. Carve your design using tools similar to those on page 77. If the sand mix is still fairly soft, cut it with a knife. As the concrete hardens, a rasp works better.

The tradition of shaping concrete to resemble wood dates back to at least the 1880s, when French artisans used the technique for garden seats, railings, planters, and trellises that today are considered fine antiques. The craftsmen applied a sand mix to

A faux bois planter

metal mesh or metal armatures and carved the details by hand. Today, you can still make faux bois ("fake wood," in French) this way, but the method shown here is easier. You simply paint a mold material onto actual wood, wait for it to cure, and then peel it off to create a reverse shape that you can use to mold concrete. We used a thick paint-on product sold at pottery-supply companies (see Resources). This material stands up to the alkalinity of cement, so you can cast many duplicates. If you want to make only one or two casts, you can use paint-on latex mold material, which is sold at some crafts and art-supply stores. Mold materials are messy and many create fumes you do not want to breathe. Work outdoors.

DIRECTIONS

1 For a planter, cut a section of a log and brush the bark free of moss and debris. Roll out a piece of potter's clay to make a pad that extends about an inch beyond the end of the log. Push the wider end of the wood into the clay and form the excess clay into a smooth lip. This will shape the top rim of your pot. If your mold material is compatible with petroleum jelly, use it as a mold release. Brush on a thick layer and heat with a hair dryer just until the brushstrokes melt and merge.

2 If your mold material is a two-part product, cut disposable plastic drinking cups to about ½-cup size. (It's easier to measure accurately by determining when these cups are full than to fill up to a line.) Wearing gloves, measure the components as specified on the package. Use separate spatulas to scrape the cupfuls into a clear plastic cup. Mix thoroughly with a third spatula. Pour into a fresh plastic cup and stir again. Avoid creating bubbles. Look through the plastic to make sure there are no streaks.

3 With a disposable plastic-bristle brush, coat the greased wood with the mixture. Aim for a thorough coat, not a thick one. While you wait for the mold material to stiffen, wipe off the spatulas so you can reuse them.

Tip

IF YOU HAVE SLABS OF BARK, you can use this technique to cast faux bois steppingstones. They look especially at home in a woodland setting.

4 Prepare a fresh batch of mold material using new plastic cups for mixing containers. Spread over the mold with a spatula. While the material is still soft, smooth short pieces of nylon stocking over the surface and press gently to embed the mesh. The nylon reinforces the mold, protecting against tears.

5 Mix a third batch, again using fresh containers. Coat the surface, paying particular attention to any parts that appear thin. If you see bubbles in the earlier layers, break them and recoat. Put extra mold material around the base so that you have a firm edge.

6 The next day, when the mold material is no longer tacky, carefully peel it from the wood as though you were removing a stocking. Turn the mold so that the wood texture faces inward.

7 To complete the mold, find a suitable container to shape the inside surface of your planter. We made one from cardboard and tape and filled it with sand for stiffening. If you are casting a round planter, a yogurt container or similar tub will work well.

8 Prepare Basic Sand Mix, page 52, or a bagged sand mix using concrete bonding adhesive in place of half the water unless the package specifies adding only water. Add pigment, if you wish. Fill the bottom of the mold and jiggle it to settle the mix and raise bubbles. Insert a piece of plastic pipe just long enough to extend through the bottom of the pot to create a drain hole, if desired. Then add the interior mold and finish filling. Tamp as you go, using a stick that fits between the two molds.

9 Create a smooth edge on the finished planter. With a putty knife or another tool, smooth the top edge. To round it slightly cut into the sand mix at an angle along the edges, then smooth the top surface again.

Garden decorations

BELOW: *Two concrete fish add a touch of whimsy to a lovely garden path.*

USING CONCRETE, YOU CAN CREATE MANY DIFFERENT TYPES OF GARDEN ORNAMENTS, including fountains, stands for gazing globes or sundials, and whimsical features that you form in molds you improvise. Keep your eyes open and you'll find clever uses for old rubber gloves, old boots, even old light fixtures. Just remember that molds must either be flexible or they must be free of undercut areas—parts where the mold would be impossible to remove once the concrete hardens. If you use flexible molds, you'll need to support them fully while the concrete stiffens.

178

OPPOSITE, TOP: *Simple geometric shapes were combined in an unusual way to create this stunning garden bench.*

ABOVE, LEFT: *Because concrete is heavy and rotproof, it makes an ideal base for many garden decorations, such as this sundial.*

ABOVE, RIGHT: *You can boost the effect of small concrete features by grouping them. This cherub oversees a water bowl.*

RIGHT: *A tapered pillar of tinted concrete and two pieces of copper pipe soldered together produce an unusual fountain that would be at home in a wide range of gardens.*

This fountain consists of two parts: a back piece molded to the impression left by cattails pressed into potter's clay and a tub adorned with water-lily pads. We cast piping into the back piece, hiding all the tubing, but for an even simpler project you can

A garden fountain

string a hose from the tub through foliage and around the back to the spout. Either way, you won't need any holes in the tub. To keep the back from tipping, bolt it to the tub above the water line. If you have access to a hammer drill and masonry bit,

you can drill the bolt holes after you cast the parts. Otherwise, create the necessary holes as you pour the concrete, the method we show here.

DIRECTIONS

1 Buy the pump first so you know how deep your tub needs to be. Our tub is 24 inches long, 14 inches wide, and 9 inches deep on the outside. Build interior and exterior forms and shape reinforcing, as shown for the sink on page 124, but omit the plumbing details. Notch the base to make a lip that will brace the fountain's back piece.

2 Add a T-brace (sold with builder's hardware) so you can bolt the back to the tub later. Thread 1-inch-long carriage bolts through the two lower holes on the brace and through small holes in the reinforcing cage and add washers and nuts. This allows you to cast the brace into the tub wall.

3 To cast water-lily decorations into the front of the tub, cut shapes from cardboard or foam core and glue them to the mold. We used foam core.

4 Prepare Basic Sand Mix, page 52, or a bagged sand mix. Replace half the mix water with acrylic or latex fortifier. This makes the tub more waterproof. Fill the mold as shown for the sink. First, fill the bottom halfway; then, insert the reinforcing cage and finish filling the bottom. Insert the interior mold and fill the sides. Tap the mold every half-inch or so to work out air gaps. Align the T-brace so that it is flush with the interior of the tub. Fill in behind it, working the mix around the bolts. Smooth the top edge.

5 Cover with plastic and keep damp for several days before removing the forms. To free the interior, remove screws and cut away the foam in layers. A small prybar helps, but don't use it against the concrete.

6 Design the back in a size that fits with your tub. Ours is 36 inches tall, 14 inches wide, and 3¼ inches thick. (If you don't cast the piping into the concrete, make it just 2 inches thick.) Cut the form from melamine-coated particleboard. Before you assemble the pieces, slice ½-inch-thick pieces of potter's clay and roll them into a smooth sheet over the bottom of the form. Trim the edges, leaving a gap if you want to create a frame.

7 Arrange cattails or other suitable decoration on the clay. Use a stub of pipe to stand in for the waterspout so that you can place the other elements around it. The back will sit within the tub, so your design will emerge from the water.

8 Test your decorative materials on a scrap of clay to see whether you must spray them with oil to prevent the clay from sticking. Cattails were fine without it. Press the decorations into the clay. Use a potter's tool or a chopstick where your fingers are too big. Then remove the pieces and spray the clay with cooking oil. If you aren't adding concrete immediately, cover the mold tightly with plastic wrap, then with a plastic bag.

9 Screw the mold together and assemble piping for the fountain. The pump we bought calls for ½-inch tubing, so we used a barbed connector to link a section of underwater tubing with cast-in-place ½-inch CPVC piping. (Standard ½-inch PVC is too thick to hide in concrete this thick.) A couple of 90-degree elbows completed the setup.

10 Using the actual molded tub, make a template from sturdy cardboard or thin plywood to show you exactly where to place the bolt that will connect the back to the T-brace. For reinforcing, cut several pieces of ¼-inch threaded rod 2 inches shorter than the back.

11 Prepare more sand mix. Fill the form using the patty procedure shown on page 108. Take care not to move the piping. When the mold is full, place pencil rods on the surface, spacing them equally starting 1 inch from the sides. Avoid placing rods near the piping. Tamp in, as shown on page 159. Using the template, insert the head end of a bolt with a washer and wiggle the bolt to embed it. Only threads, wrapped with tape, should project from the concrete.

12 Keep damp several days. Remove the mold. Brush and rinse off any stuck clay and fill holes with a paste of cement and water. Highlight raised areas on the backsplash by painting them with diluted latex paint. Bolt on the back-splash. Fill the tub to create an anchor weight.

183

A garden pedestal makes a good base for a birdbath, gazing globe, sundial, or garden pot. This version has a sculptural look thanks to the way it is built. The main skeleton is a cylindrical form usually used in pouring foundations. Wrapped with hardware cloth

A garden pedestal

and expanded-metal lath, it provides a good base for a cement-and-sand mixture, which glitters in the sun because handfuls of mother-of-pearl were pressed into the surface. The pedestal can support a relatively light load, such as a sundial or globe.

DIRECTIONS

1 First, cut pieces for the skeleton. With a fine-tooth saw, cut a 6-inch-diameter cardboard cylinder 36 inches long. To make a base cone, cut a semicircle of expanded-metal lath. Create the shape by marking two positions as you rotate a stick around a pivot point 28 inches from the end of the sheet. Make one set of marks 9 inches down and the second 27½ inches down. Cut along the two curves with aviator's snips. To wrap the top of the tube, cut one piece of hardware cloth 24 by 24 inches.

2 Using 20-gauge galvanized wire, stitch the lath into a cone and the hardware cloth into a tube. Weave in and out with needle-nose pliers when necessary. Slip the cone and then the tube onto the cardboard and stitch the two metal pieces together. There will be extra hardware cloth at the top. Snip tabs into the excess at the top and fold them in. Stitch with wire.

3 Plaster the form with Basic Sand Mix, page 52, or a bagged sand mix prepared quite stiff. Load the mix onto an inverted trowel, as if it were a mason's hod, and gently push small amounts onto the mesh. Don't attempt to smooth the surface—the next layer sticks better if it's rough. Cover with plastic until the concrete stiffens.

4 Paint the surface with concrete bonding adhesive.

5 Apply the second coat by hand. Pat or trowel it smooth.

6 Add sparkle by pressing mother-of-pearl into the top layer while it is pliable. Dampen the shells first so they don't soak up water from the surrounding cement mix.

Projects from improvised molds

Basically, you can use almost anything that's relatively nonporous as long as it's either stiff or can be fortified to hold heavy concrete without flexing. For the globes shown above, we used old light fixtures as molds. After packing them with a basic sand mix, we inserted dowel stubs in the bases and waited a week before breaking the glass (over a bucket) with a hammer. We drilled matching dowel holes in a post and a rock, and—voilà!—we had garden art. For the mother-of-pearl decoration, smear glue on the inside of the glass and press on the inlays, then add sand mix. The next page shows some of the other ideas that struck our fancy.

SCARECROW

This curious garden guard gets its shape from a variety of found molds plus flexible copper pipe. The face comes from a plastic mask sold at craft stores. A plastic bag set into a bed of sand shaped the rounded back of the head. After the sand mix set, we drilled recesses for the eyes and glued on marbles. We used rubber boots to shape the feet and disposable vinyl gloves, with a wire poked down each finger, for the hands. We inserted a copper coupling into the wet sand mix at the base or top of each mold.

POST HOLDER

An oversize plastic funnel makes a handy mold for an anchor to hold garden ornaments or signs. We glued bits of recycled bottle glass to the inside of the funnel and taped the tip shut. Then we placed the mold (tip side down) in a wide can and filled the funnel with a concrete mix. A few days later, we tipped the concrete out and drilled a matching tapered hole in the post. To create the taper, we used progressively smaller spade bits.

EDGING

To create curb or edging pieces suitable for lining garden beds, paths, and parking areas, we stuck pieces of glazed tile to squares of adhesive shelf paper and placed them in the bottom of a plastic tray sold for wetting sheets of wallpaper. We hooked a couple of clamps over the edges to keep the tray's thin sides from flaring out, then added Basic Concrete Mix and jiggled it to release air bubbles.

DECORATIVE TILE

This lacy tile began as part of a doormat. We sprayed the mat with cooking oil and placed it upside down in the bottom of a box built of melamine-coated particleboard. (A plywood form or one made from cardboard will also work.) Then it's just a matter of adding Basic Concrete Mix or Basic Sand Mix (page 52). A tile like this can be used on a path or patio, but it's decorative enough to stand on its own as garden art. Adding a spout will turn it into a backsplash for a garden fountain.

RESOURCES

If you're ready to go ahead with a decorative concrete project, you'll find most of the materials you need at local home-improvement stores. For a wider assortment of pigments, white cement, and special aggregate, look in the phone book under "Concrete—Ready-Mixed." Even though companies listed there most likely sell concrete by the truckload, they usually sell related materials in small quantities or can recommend where to get them. Here's a start on some additional sources of supplies and information. Most of the specialty companies ship nationwide.

TECHNICAL INFORMATION

Brickform® Blush-Tone Acid Stain™
Rancho Cucamonga, CA
(800) 483-9628
www.brickform.com

Cast Stone Institute
Lawrenceville, GA
(770) 972-3011
www.caststone.org

Portland Cement Association
Skokie, IL
(847) 966-6200
www.cement.org

ACID STAIN

Colormaker Floors Ltd.
Vancouver, BC, Canada
(888) 875-9425
www.colormakerfloors.com

Kemiko
Leonard, TX
(903) 587-3708
www.kemiko.com

L. M. Scofield Co.
Douglasville, GA
Los Angeles, CA
(800) 800-9900
www.scofield.com

ADDITIVES

Cheng Concrete Exchange
Oakland, CA
(510) 849-3272
www.concreteexchange.com

Fritz-Pak Concrete Additives
Dallas, TX
(888) 746-4116
www.fritzpak.com

The Concrete Countertop Institute
(Metakaolin in small quantities)
Raleigh, NC
(888) 386-7711
www.concretecountertop institute.com

AGGREGATE

Heritage Glass
Smithfield, UT
(435) 563-5585
heritageglass.net

Manufacturers Mineral Co.
Renton, WA
(425) 228-2120

Mesolini Glass Studio
Bainbridge Island, WA
(206) 842-7133
www.mesolini.com

Spectrum Glass Co., Inc.
Woodinville, WA
(425) 483-6699
www.spectrumglass.com

Terrazzo & Stone Supply Co.
Bellevue, WA
(888) 644-5577
Marysville, WA
(877) 534-4477
www.terrazzostone.com

BAGGED MIXES

Buddy Rhodes Concrete Counter Mix
Buddy Rhodes Studio
San Francisco, CA
(877) 706-5303
www.buddyrhodes.com

EnCounter Professional Countertop System
Oklahoma City, OK
(866) 906-2006
www.encountertop.com

LifeTime Elements Quicktops
Hudson, WI
(877) 386-8786
www.lifetimefloors.biz

Quikrete
The Quikrete Companies
Atlanta, GA
(800) 282-5828
www.quikrete.com

Sakrete
Bonsal American
Charlotte, NC
(800) 334-0784
www.bonsal.com

BRASS AND NICKEL GAUGE STRIPS

Terrazzo & Stone Supply Co.
Bellevue, WA
(888) 644-5577
Marysville, WA
(877) 534-4477
www.terrazzostone.com

CLASSES AND HOW-TO VIDEOS

Buddy Rhodes Concrete Products
San Francisco, CA
(877) 706-5303
www.buddyrhodes.com

Concrete Countertop Institute
Raleigh, NC
(888) 386-7711
www.concretecountertop institute.com

Decorative Concrete Institute
(Staining, stamping, overlays)
Temple, GA
(770) 562-1441
www.decorativeconcrete institute.com

LifeTime Floors Elements
(Video on fiberoptics in concrete)
Hudson, WI
(877) 386-8786
www.lifetimefloors.biz

School of Faux Rock Construction
Amity, OR
(888) 684-0086
www.jpjtechnologies.com

Yestermorrow Design/ Build School
Warren, VT
(888) 496-5541
www.yestermorrow.org

COLOR HARDENER

L. M. Scofield Co.
Douglasville, GA
Los Angeles, CA
(800) 800-9900
www.scofield.com

CONCRETE: CUSTOM AND READY-MADE FOR HOME AND GARDEN

Absolute Concrete Works
Poulsbo, WA
(360) 297-5055
www.absoluteconcrete works.com

Architectural Concrete Specialties
Phoenix, AZ
(480) 921-3826
www.acsconcrete.com

Art & Maison, Inc.
North Miami, FL
(305) 948-0477
www.artandmaison.com

Artisans Concrete Supply
(360) 509-8651

Bomanite Corporation
Madera, CA
(559) 673-2411
www.bomanite.com

Buddy Rhodes Studio
San Francisco, CA
(877) 706-5303
www.buddyrhodes.com

Colorado Concrete Concepts
Denver, CO
(720) 374-2101
www.coloradoconcrete concepts.com

Concrete Central
New York, NY
(917) 991-2031
www.concretecentral.net

Concreteworks Studio
Oakland, CA and Helmetta, NJ
(510) 534-7141
www.concreteworks.com

Counter Production
(Concrete with recycled glass)
Berkeley, CA
(510) 843-6916
www.counterproduction.com

DEX Studios
Atlanta, GA
(404) 753-0600
www.dexstudios.com

Dogpaw Design
Seattle, WA
(206) 706-0099
www.dogpaw.com

Flying Turtle Cast Concrete
Modesto, CA
(209) 530-1611
www.flyingturtlecast
concrete.com

**Form/Function Custom
Concrete**
Rowley, MA
(978) 432-1093
www.formfunction
concrete.com

Grotto Designs
Canmore, Alberta, Canada
(866) 262-3966
www.grottodesigns.com

Meld USA
Raleigh, NC
(919) 790-1749
www.meldusa.com

Nichols Bros. Stoneworks
Snohomish, WA
(800) 483-5720
www.nicholsbros.com

Omer Arbel Design Office
(Ductal concrete chair)
Vancouver, BC, Canada
(604) 818-1880
www.omerarbel.com

Oso Industries
Brooklyn, NY
(347) 365-0389
www.osoindustries.com

Prettyhard Fine Concrete
Charlottesville, VA
(434) 296-0755
www.prettyhard.com

R&A Concrete
Arlington, WA
(360) 435-3885
www.raconcrete.com

Robyn Krutch
Bainbridge Island, WA
(206) 842-1121

Sonoma Cast Stone
Sonoma, CA
(888) 807-4234
www.sonomastone.com

Stone Soup Concrete
Florence, MA
(800) 819-3456
www.stonesoupconcrete.com

Syndesis Inc.
Santa Monica, CA
(310) 829-9932
www.syndesisinc.com

Topher Delaney Studios
San Francisco, CA
(415) 621-9899
www.tdelaney.com

CONTRACTOR LISTINGS
www.concretenetwork.com
www.decorative-concrete.net
www.concreteexchange.com

Floor Seasons
Las Vegas, NV
(702) 348-8971
www.floorseasons.com

**Water Brothers
Construction Inc.**
Eugene, OR
(541) 729-8563
www.walerbrothers.com

DYE
Brickform® Dye-N-Seal™
Rancho Cucamonga, CA
(800) 483-9628
www.brickform.com

**FIBEROPTICS
FOR CONCRETE**
LifeTime Floors Elements
(How-to video and custom
countertops)
Hudson, WI
(877) 386-8786
www.lifetimefloors.biz

Kiesub Electronics
Las Vegas, NV
(702) 733-0024
www.kiesub.com

**GARDEN POTS
AND SCULPTURE**
Nichols Bros. Stoneworks
Snohomish, WA
(800) 483-5720
www.nicholsbros.com

Robyn Krutch
Bainbridge Island, WA
(206) 842-1121

**LIGHT-TRANSMISSIBLE
CONCRETE**
LiTraCon Bt.
H-6640 Csongrád
Tanya 832
Hungary
011-36-30-255-1648
www.litracon.hu

MOLDS
History Stones
Camas, WA
(360) 834-7021
www.historystones.com

**PAINT-ON MOLD
MATERIAL**
Por-A-Mold
Synair Corporation
Chattanooga, TN
(800) 251-7642
www.synair.com

**PEAL-AWAY
STAIN-RESIST GEL**
**LesCoat Concrete
Stain Block**
Lansdale, PA
(866) 906-2006
www.stenciledconcrete
stains.com

PIGMENTS
B&J Colorants
(Including bronze pigment)
Marietta, GA
(770) 951-8686
blueconcrete@bellsouth.net

Buddy Rhodes Studio
San Francisco, CA
(877) 706-5303
www.buddyrhodes.com

Davis Colors
Beltsville, MD
(800) 638-4444
Los Angeles, CA
(800) 356-4848
www.daviscolors.com

EnColor
Oklahoma City, OK
(866) 906-2006
www.encountertop.com

Interstar
Junction City, IL
(800) 567-1857
www.interstar.ca/concrete

QC Construction Products
Madera, CA
(800) 453-8213
www.qcconprod.com

Solomon Colors
Springfield, IL
(800) 624-0261
www.solomoncolors.com

POLISHING TOOLS
Granite City Tool Co.
St. Cloud, MN
(800) 328-7094
www.granitecitytool.com

Master Wholesale, Inc.
Seattle, WA
(800) 938-7925
www.masterwholesale.com

**MESH AND FIBER
REINFORCEMENT**
Nippon Electric Glass
(Alkali-resistant glass fibers)
Grand Prairie, TX
(972) 602-1740
www.negamerica.com

Synthetic Industries, Inc.
Chattanooga, TN
(800) 635-2308
www.fibermesh.com

TechFab, LLC
(Carbon fiber C-Grid™)
Anderson, SC
(864) 260-3355
www.techfabllc.com

**VERTICAL STAMPING
MIXES, TOOLS, AND TIPS**
FossilCrete
Oklahoma City, OK
(405) 525-3722
www.fossilcrete.com

Flex-C-Ment
Greer, SC
(864) 877-3111
www.flex-c-ment.com

WHITE CEMENT
Lehigh Cement Co.
Allentown, PA
(800) 523-5488
www.lehighwhitecement.com

DESIGN & PHOTOGRAPHY

INDEX

INDEX (continued)